DECADES

Fleetwood Mac

in the 1970s

Andrew Wild

sonicbondpublishing.com

Sonicbond Publishing Limited
www.sonicbondpublishing.co.uk
Email: info@sonicbondpublishing.co.uk

First Published in the United Kingdom 2021
First Published in the United States 2021

British Library Cataloguing in Publication Data:
A Catalogue record for this book is available from the British Library

Typeset in ITC Garamond & ITC Avant Garde
Printed and bound in England

Graphic design and typesetting: Full Moon Media

In Memorium

Bob Brunning (29 June 1943 – 18 October 2011)
Bob Welch (31 August 1945 – 7 June 2012)
Bob Weston (1 November 1947 – circa 3 January 2012)
Danny Kirwan (13 May 1950 – 8 June 2018)
Peter Green (29 October 1946 – 25 July 2020)

Mick Fleetwood:
I could have never planned any of this. I don't even believe in making plans. They only create an atmosphere of disappointment. So it's not a day-to-day situation with us, but there's always full potential of either great things happening or totally disastrous things happening. Fleetwood Mac, from point one, has been like that.

John McVie:
The whole story of Fleetwood Mac is one of happenstance. Luck, coincidence, kismet, fate, karma. A whole host of incidents that no one planned or expected.

With much love to Amanda, Rosie and Amy.
Thank you, Martin Schreiber. Special thanks to Nick Jackson.

Also by Andrew Wild

Local History
108 Steps Around Macclesfield (Sigma Press, 1994 / 2nd edition, Rumble Strips, 2018)
Exploring Chester (Sigma Press, 1996 / re-publication, Rumble Strips, 2018)
Ever Forward (MADS, 1997)

Biographies
Play On (Twelfth Night, 2009)
One for the Record (Avalon, 2013 / 2nd edition, 2018)

Music
Pink Floyd Song by Song (Fonthill, 2017)
Queen On Track (Sonicbond, 2018)
The Beatles: An A-Z Guide to Every Song (Sonicbond, 2019)
Solo Beatles 1969-1980 On Track (Sonicbond, 2020)
Crosby, Stills and Nash On Track (Sonicbond, 2020)
Dire Straits On Track (Sonicbond, 2021)
Eric Clapton Solo On Track (Sonicbond, 2021)

Films
James Bond On Screen (Sonicbond, 2021)

Plays
The Difficult Crossing (Stagescripts, 2016)

DECADES | Fleetwood Mac in the 1970s

Contents

Would you like to write for Sonicbond Publishing?

We are mainly a music publisher, but we also occasionally publish in other genres including film and television. At Sonicbond Publishing we are always on the look-out for authors, particularly for our two main series, On Track and Decades.

Mixing fact with in depth analysis, the On Track series examines the entire recorded work of a particular musical artist or group. All genres are considered from easy listening and jazz to 60s soul to 90s pop, via rock and metal.

The Decades series singles out a particular decade in an artist or group's history and focuses on that decade in more detail than may be allowed in the On Track series.

While professional writing experience would, of course, be an advantage, the most important qualification is to have real enthusiasm and knowledge of your subject. First-time authors are welcomed, but the ability to write well in English is essential.

Sonicbond Publishing has distribution throughout Europe and North America, and all our books are also published in E-book form. Authors will be paid a royalty based on sales of their book.

Further details about our books are available from www.sonicbondpublishing.com. To contact us, complete the contact form there or email info@sonicbondpublishing.co.uk

Author's Note

Unless stated otherwise, all Mick Fleetwood quotes are from *Play On: Now, Then, and Fleetwood Mac*; Jeremy Spencer quotes are from a 2011 interview with Michael Limnios published on *blues. gr*; Dave Walker, Peter Green, Clifford Davis, John McVie, Bob Welch, Bob Weston, Walter Egan and Keith Olsen quotes are from interviews at *fleetwoodmac.net*; Carol Ann Harris quotes are from *My Life with Lindsey Buckingham and Fleetwood Mac*; Ken Caillat quotes are from *Making Rumours: The Inside Story of the Classic Fleetwood Mac Album* and *Get Tusked: The Inside Story of Fleetwood Mac's Most Anticipated Album*.

Introduction

Music fans tend to divide into two camps when you mention Fleetwood Mac – those who think of the multi-million-selling five-piece that formed in the mid-1970s and released one of the biggest selling albums of all time; and those who adopt a self-appointed 'cooler' stance, preferring the late-'60s blues band fronted by the virtuosic guitarist, Peter Green.

But that's not the whole story. Or anything close. Between May 1970 – when Green left his own band to be replaced by the bass player's wife – to the beginning of 1975 when Lindsey Buckingham and Stevie Nicks joined Fleetwood Mac, there were almost five years of what can only be described as turmoil. One by one, talented musicians such as Jeremy Spencer, Danny Kirwan, Bob Weston and Bob Welch joined and left Fleetwood Mac. They were a six-piece at the end of 1972, a trio by the end of 1974.

Whilst it's impossible to ignore the skill and longevity of such classic songs as 'The Chain', 'Dreams', 'Don't Stop', 'Gold Dust Woman', 'Go Your Own Way', 'Over My Head', 'Rhiannon', 'Sara', 'Say You Love Me', 'Second Hand News', 'Tusk' and 'You Make Loving Fun': from *Fleetwood Mac* (1975), *Rumours* (1977) and *Tusk* (1979), there are an equal number of half-forgotten classic songs from the first half of the 1970s, such as 'Dust', 'The Green Manalishi (With The Two Prong Crown)', 'Hypnotised', 'Jewel-Eyed Judy', 'Sentimental Lady', 'Spare Me A Little Of Your Love', 'Station Man', 'Sunny Side Of Heaven' and 'World in Harmony'.

Here then, is the story of Fleetwood Mac in the 1970s – the music, the people, the tours, the rumours, the failures and the successes.

Men's Journal in 2014:

John married Christine. Lindsey slept with Stevie. Mick slept with Stevie. Christine divorced John and slept with the lighting director and then with Beach Boy, Dennis Wilson. John stayed drunk for decades. Stevie hit cocaine and Kolonopin. Christine retreated to an English country farm. Mick went broke. Lindsey threw misunderstood-genius tantrums that ended with his slapping Stevie and leaving the band for nine years. The one constant has been Mick Fleetwood, both enabler and protector.

Strap in.

Andrew Wild
Rainow, Cheshire, March 2021

Prelude 1967-1969: Coming Your Way

At the beginning of 1970, Fleetwood Mac had existed for two and a half years. They were founded in London in July 1967 by guitarist Peter Green and drummer Mick Fleetwood.

Green had come to rapid prominence in the influential British blues band John Mayall's Bluesbreakers. Before joining Mayall, Green had worked with Mick Fleetwood in two short-lived groups in early 1966: Peter B's Looners and Shotgun Express. He hooked up with Mayall in July that year, aged just nineteen, replacing Eric Clapton, who had just formed Cream. Green's playing was less aggressive than Clapton's but otherwise equal in every respect. And at times, better.

The Bluesbreakers line-up at that time was Mayall, Green, drummer Hughie Flint, and bassist John McVie. McVie had joined Mayall, aged seventeen, in 1963. Flint was replaced by Aynsley Dunbar in September 1966 and this line-up recorded the album *A Hard Road*, released in February 1967. Green's instrumental, 'The Supernatural', is a charged, emotional showcase for his significant skills as a blues guitarist and a template for his subsequent work with Fleetwood Mac. Green's tone and control on 'Someday After A While (You'll Be Sorry)' is as good as anything Eric Clapton performed with Mayall or anyone else. The obscure B-side, 'Out of Reach', sung by Green, is better still: a magnificent, despondent blues classic with a tortured vocal and icy, reverberant guitar tone. Both *A Hard Road* and its predecessor *Bluesbreakers with Eric Clapton*, achieved top ten chart placings in the UK.

Dunbar left in April 1967, and nineteen-year-old Mick Fleetwood occupied the drum stool for around six weeks in mid-April and May. A number of live recordings of Mayall's band were made between 1 February and 5 May 1967 at Brixton's Ram Jam, Hampstead's Klooks Kleek and Soho's Marquee, and some of these were released in 2016 as *Live in 1967*. Although exact recording dates and the extent of Fleetwood's precise tenure with Mayall's band cannot be determined, these might include the earliest available recordings of Mick Fleetwood and John McVie playing together.

The genesis of Fleetwood Mac can be definitively pinpointed to 19 April 1967, when Green, McVie and Fleetwood recorded two songs at the Decca Studios in West Hampstead. The session was a gift from John Mayall and followed on from the recording of a new Bluesbreakers single: 'Double Trouble' b/w 'It Hurts Me Too', released on 2 June.

'Mayall had bought Greenie a few hours of studio time as a birthday gift so that he could record some songs he had written', Mick Fleetwood says, although Green had celebrated his twentieth birthday the previous October. 'We were recorded by Gus Dudgeon, the Decca house engineer who went on to become extremely famous for his work with Elton John.'

The instrumental, 'Fleetwood Mac', was named for Fleetwood and McVie. The other song recorded was the astounding 'First Train Home'. Fleetwood was sacked by Mayall in May 1967. Green left a few weeks later, on 15 June 1967, hooking up once more with Mick Fleetwood. Fleetwood said later:

> A few weeks after I'd been ejected from the Bluesbreakers, Peter Green gave in his notice. He'd had enough. His initial plans didn't involve forming a new band, but his agency persuaded him and he came round to see me… and between us, we got Fleetwood Mac together. At that time, we had no manager, so we did everything ourselves – got the van and equipment sorted out – and Peter did all the negotiation with Blue Horizon Records.

John McVie was not prepared to risk his weekly income; therefore Bob Brunning was the band's first bass player.

'I answered an ad in the *Melody Maker* for a bass player', he recalled later, 'and got the job'.

Brunning had recorded three singles with Five's Company. Other bass players known to have applied, include Dave Ambrose (who'd played with Green and Fleetwood in Shotgun Express), future Family and Blind Faith bassist, Ric Grech (who rehearsed a few times with the band but declined to join), and Bruce Thomas, later of Elvis Costello and the Attractions.

Fleetwood Mac signed with Mike Vernon's Blue Horizon record label. Vernon had produced John Mayall's recent albums and the first recordings by a young David Bowie. Uncertain about his skills as a frontman, Green wanted to recruit a second guitarist in Fleetwood Mac to divert some of the spotlight away from him. Nineteen-year-old, Jeremy Spencer, was poached from a band called the Levi Set Blues Band.

In 2015, Tim Sommer of *The Observer* memorably described Spencer as 'an elfin devotee of amphetamine rockabilly whose persona seems to presage Dr. Feelgood'.

Green and Vernon had met Spencer during Green's last days with John

Mayall, as Spencer recalls:

In early spring of 1967, the Levi Set – consisting of John Charles on bass, his brother Ian on drums and myself on guitar – received a surprise announcement from a friend, Phil Smith, that we were to be auditioned by none other than Mike Vernon. Phil had written in answer to an advertisement in Melody Maker which said that Mike Vernon was to be scouting the British Isles for blues talent and to contact him if anyone was interested or knew of a band or musicians who would fit the bill. Phil told him about this little fellow in Lichfield who played and sang like Elmore James. Mike travelled up to Wall – a tiny village outside Lichfield – where we had set up in the local hall. We did a thirty-minute set, and Mike was impressed and enthusiastic. He returned a couple of weeks later with a tape recorder to get some of our stuff down. Mike told me that Peter Green was quitting John Mayall in order to form his own band and wanted to find another guitarist. So he arranged for us to play for half an hour between the sets of an upcoming John Mayall gig at Birmingham's Le Metro club (11 June 1967) so that Pete could see and hear me play. I walked up to Peter and introduced myself: well, I was about to introduce myself. He said 'Jeremy? Jeremy Spencer?' before I said anything. 'Yes', I said. 'Do you listen to Elmore James?' He said, 'Yes, all the time. Do you listen to B. B. King?'. I said, 'Yes', and we chatted until it came time for their set. The Levi Set played for about half an hour (between Mayall's sets) and Peter played harmonica on the first number: 'Dust My Broom'. After their second set, Pete asked if I wanted a drink, and we stood by the bar, where he talked as though I was already in the band! He was saying stuff like, 'Well, you can do a couple of Elmore things and then I do a couple of BB's and so on like that…'. I finally said, 'Are you serious? Do you like what I play?'. He said that I was the first guitarist that made him smile since Hendrix! Can you believe it? Then he showed me a page that he had written in his notebook while on his way up to Birmingham. It was like a prayer that said something like, 'I can't go on with this music like it is. Please have Jeremy be good, please have him be good'.

'Mick and I went to see Jeremy play one night', Peter Green recalled years later, 'and asked him to join us'.

The Green-Fleetwood-Spencer-Brunning line-up made its debut on 13 August 1967 at the Windsor Jazz and Blues Festival. They were billed as 'Peter Green's Fleetwood Mac, featuring Jeremy Spencer'. According to Spencer, Green chose to call his band Fleetwood Mac because he expected McVie to join up before long and that, in the longer term, he could leave and they would still have their names as part of the band's moniker. John McVie was in attendance at Windsor: John Mayall's Bluesbreakers were on the bill and McVie watched Fleetwood Mac's set from the side of the stage.

'We knew he was there', Mick Fleetwood recalls. 'In fact, to me it felt like we were auditioning for him. It was the moment that John more or less decided to join us.'

And that wasn't all. Also appearing at the festival were Cream featuring Eric Clapton, and Birmingham blues band Chicken Shack, who had a soulful vocalist and piano player called Christine Perfect. Christine remembered in *Pete Frame's Rock Family Trees* in 1979:

Mike Vernon wanted to sign (Chicken Shack) to Blue Horizon, but thought they needed a pianist. So I joined as pianist and alternate vocalist (usually when Stan needed to catch his breath). I'd moved down to London because I thought I'd find a lot more fun down there; I certainly had no aspirations as a musician at that time – in fact, I'd forgotten all about it. But all of a sudden, I found myself listening to a pile of Freddie King records, trying to pick up what I could of his piano player's (Sonny Thompson's) style. Then we went off and did five sets a night at the Star Club in Hamburg for a month before making our British debut at the Windsor Festival in August 1967… which is where I first ran into Fleetwood Mac.

Bob Brunning played a handful of gigs with Fleetwood Mac before John McVie decided his future lay with Green and Fleetwood, finally joining in September 1967. He told *Record World*:

I thought that Mayall was getting too jazzy, after he brought about three horns in. We were doing a gig in Norwich, and we did a soundcheck, working some arrangement out – this was when I was still a very hardcore blues addict, with the 'There is nothing outside of the blues' attitude. So one of the horn players asked, 'What kind of solo do you want in this section?' And I'll always remember, John said, 'Oh, just play free-form.' I thought to myself, 'Okay, that's it.' We used to do two sets, so during the interval, I went out and phoned up Greenie and said, 'Hey, you need a bass player? I'm in.'

'Once we had John McVie, we were a tight musical juggernaut, off and running', says Mick Fleetwood. Bob Brunning: 'I thoroughly enjoyed my brief time in Fleetwood Mac, and remained friendly with them all. People often ask me how I feel about it. I actually got 'promotion' at the time. I joined Savoy Brown, who were working three times as hard and made a lot more money!'.

Fleetwood Mac's first album was recorded, in the main, completely live, over several sessions at CBS Studios in London, in November and December 1967. One track – recorded earlier at Decca Studios in September – features Bob Brunning. Released in February 1968, the album was a big hit, spending more than six months in the UK top 20. It peaked twice at number 4 in April and July 1968, in the wake of the singles 'Black Magic Woman' – a latin-influenced Peter Green rewrite of Otis Rush's 'All Your Love', which Green had performed with John Mayall – and 'Need Your Love So Bad'.

Fleetwood Mac quickly established themselves as a formidable live act, playing the club circuit at famous venues such as The Marquee, the Roundhouse and Middle Earth in London, and the Ricky Tick in Windsor. It was after a gig at the Ricky Tick that John McVie asked out Christine Perfect. They would marry that summer. At the time, she admits she was more interested in Peter Green, as she told *Rolling Stone* in 1977:

> I went to see Fleetwood Mac one night. John didn't have his girlfriend ... He asked me if I wanted to have a drink, and we sat down, had a few laughs, then they had to go onstage. All the time, I was kind of eyeballing ol' Greenie. After the concert was over, John came over and said, 'Shall I take you out to dinner sometime?'. I went, 'Whoa... I thought you were engaged or something'. He said, 'Nah, it's all over'. I thought he was devastatingly attractive, but it had never occurred to me to look at him.

Fleetwood Mac's second album, *Mr. Wonderful*, was recorded in April 1968, once again at CBS Studios in London. Released that August, it was an all-blues album, like their debut. Christine Perfect guested on piano.

'We knew she was a great piano player', Mick Fleetwood recalls, 'but even so, she blew us away'.

Peter Green agrees: 'I always thought that Christine's piano-playing was soft and gentle. She was great to play with and always listened to the other musicians. I have never compared her to anyone else'.

Mr. Wonderful – like its predecessor – hit the UK top ten. But it was a non-album single recorded in October 1968 that secured their long-term future. 'Albatross' is a gorgeous, timeless instrumental. The feel and mood are pure Peter Green: a cross between his earlier 'The Supernatural', Chuck Berry's 'Deep Feeling' (1957) and Santo and Johnny's 'Sleep Walk' (1957). The second guitarist on 'Albatross' is not Jeremy Spencer, however, but eighteen-year-old Londoner Danny Kirwan. Kirwan, with his band Boilerhouse, had played a few support slots for Fleetwood Mac. Peter Green was impressed enough to invite Kirwan to join Fleetwood Mac as their third guitarist.

'Danny was looking for some musicians to form his own band', Green recalled in 1999. 'We were impressed with his writing and asked him to join (us).'

Kirwan, despite his youth, was a mature and accomplished self-taught guitarist and strong songwriter. His songs and musicianship would add an important new dimension to Fleetwood Mac's sound over the next three and a half years. Recalled Jeremy Spencer:

> We'd seen him play and thought he was very good. But Peter was a little bit frustrated with me because, well, I didn't really cut it as a side guitarist – not slide, but side. Which is what Peter wanted because he backed me up on my numbers, but I didn't back him up on his! So it was understandable he needed a guitarist to back up his playing. I felt out-of-place a bit.

Kirwan's arrival and the success of 'Albatross' heralded both Fleetwood Mac's move away from pure blues, and the beginning of Jeremy Spencer's disenfranchisement with his role within the band, ultimately leading to his departure in 1971: 'I just wanted to get up there and blast away on a few Elmore songs and go home'.

Mr. Wonderful was not released in the US. About half of the songs were included in an American release called *English Rose* (January 1969), along with some new songs from Danny Kirwan. Whilst 'Albatross' sat at the top of the UK charts, Fleetwood Mac were in Chicago recording an album with Otis Spann (piano, vocals), Willie Dixon (upright bass), Shakey Horton (harmonica, vocals), J.T. Brown (tenor saxophone, vocals), Buddy Guy (guitar), Honeyboy Edwards (guitar, vocals) and S.P. Leary (drums). The double album, *Fleetwood Mac in Chicago*, would be released in December 1969. Their next single – the heartbreakingly melancholic 'Man Of The World', recorded in New York – gave Fleetwood Mac their second big hit in the UK: number 2 in June 1969. 'Man Of The World' appeared

on Immediate Records: their contract with Blue Horizon had expired and
they would shortly sign with Reprise for their next album, *Then Play On*.
In the meantime, Blue Horizon released *The Pious Bird of Good Omen*: a
collection of singles and B-sides, in August 1969.

Then Play On – recorded April to July, released in September –
prominently featured the considerable talents of Danny Kirwan. Jeremy
Spencer made virtually no contribution to this landmark album. Recalls
Mick Fleetwood:

> *Then Play On* was entirely Danny and Peter. (The album) epitomised the
> vision Peter had of going forward. Peter's songs… made the album special.
> His playing was sublime and his lyrics were expressive and poetic. Jeremy
> got left behind. Apart from a couple of piano things, he wasn't on that
> album. I didn't want to keep treading water, and that album was the real
> start of Fleetwood Mac. Peter had (however) become disillusioned with our
> success, and whatever the cause, this period of time is where the onset of
> his mental issues emerged.

The accompanying single, 'Oh Well', displayed both sides of Fleetwood
Mac – the driving, bluesy, gutbucket riffs of part one, and the gorgeously
dreamy instrumental part two. 'Oh Well' was a number 2 hit in the UK,
and crept to number 55 in the US *Billboard* listings – the band's sole
entry until 1975. 'Oh Well' is the only Fleetwood Mac song from the
1960s to stay in the band's set throughout the 1970s and beyond. It was
variously sung by Peter Green (1969-1970), Bob Welch (1971-1975), Dave
Walker (1972-1973), Lindsey Buckingham (1975-1982, 1997-2014), Billy
Burnette (1987-1995) and Mike Campbell (2018-2019).

In 1969, however, *Rolling Stone* were not convinced:

> Nowadays, Fleetwood Mac is stepping out on its own. Tired of being another
> British blues band, the group has said goodbye to Elmore James and is
> moving into the pop-rock field. On this album, they fall flat on their faces.
>
> Most of the music on the album is slow and wandering – instruments
> in search of an idea. Of the songs in this category, 'My Dream' – with its
> pleasant melody – is the only one that works. The eclecticism is excessive
> here, most of the songs sounding like warmed-over early (Country Joe
> and the) Fish, with traces of such bands as The Doors. Plus, several two-
> guitar rave-ups. Peter Green, once such a promising guitarist, is merely
> competent – nothing more, nothing less. Even the blues material is inferior

to their earlier work. To be sure, there are bits and pieces of interesting, spacey music scattered throughout the album, but it's the nondescript ramblings which dominate the set.

The best thing Fleetwood Mac has ever done is 'Oh Well', a single currently available only in England. On part one, the two guitars work with and against each other in perfect balance, and when the music pauses, there's these fine lyrics, post-Dylan, rock and roll sassy: 'I can't help it 'bout the shape I'm in/I'm not pretty, can't sing and my legs are thin/But don't ask me what I think of you/I might not give the answer that you want me to'. Part two – an instrumental – gets a bit cumbersome, but still attracts where similar songs on the album repelled. The reason this is available only in England is that the band's manager is positive that 'Rattlesnake Shake' (an album cut distinguished from the others only by the fact that it's uptempo) will hit as a single in America and on the European continent. That man is 1969's False Prophet of the Year. I'd trade this whole album straight across for 'Oh Well' and would be getting the better deal.

Many years later, they would revise their opinion. 'I think it's one of the most beautiful and exciting records ever made', *Rolling Stone* senior writer David Fricke said in 2013. 'As a statement of searching – within blues, within rock, within the possibilities of the electric guitar – it's one of the best records ever made.'

Fleetwood Mac set off on a three-month American tour in mid-November 1969.

As the seventies began, then, Fleetwood Mac's stock was high in the UK: voted 'top progressive group' in the *Melody Maker* end-of-year poll, with three top two singles since late 1968, three well-regarded top ten albums, and a burgeoning status as a crack live band.

Peter Green's biographer, Martin Celmins:

You had Peter Green playing the B.B. King-style Chicago blues, Danny Kirwan with his more melodic rock, and then Jeremy Spencer doing these remarkable Elmore James impersonations. And for all that package to be in one band, was a huge draw. And the response they got from the audience was wild. You know, they were just the top live band.

And it was as an in-concert attraction that Fleetwood Mac started their long-term assault on the US market. There would be many casualties along the way.

1970

1969-1970 American Tour

On 1 January 1970, Fleetwood Mac consisted of Peter Green, 23; Jeremy Spencer, 21; Danny Kirwan, 19; Mick Fleetwood, 22 and John McVie, the oldest at 24. They opened the year in Seattle, at the Eagle Auditorium.

The schizophrenic nature of their live set at this time is reflected in the songs they performed at a three-night residency at the Fillmore West, San Francisco, 2-4 January 1970. Covers of blues songs by Otis Rush ('Homework'), Honeyboy Edwards ('My Baby's Gone'), B.B. King ('If You Let Me Love You'), Mississippi Fred McDowell via Sam Cooke and Reverend Gary Davies ('You Gotta Move') and, inevitably, Elmore James ('Stranger Blues'), were mixed with some of their hit singles, bluesy originals such as 'Rattlesnake Shake' and 'Like it This Way', and more adventurous songs including Green's 'Before the Beginning' and Kirwan's 'Loving Kind' and 'Coming Your Way'. The power of the twin Green/Kirwan pairing is evident on recordings of these shows.

They also performed a new song, at that point unrecorded: the magnificent 'The Green Manalishi (With The Two Prong Crown)'. From its earliest arrangements, 'The Green Manalishi' would allow the band to improvise, with versions lasting twelve minutes or more. The basis of Mick Fleetwood's drum solo would later be reworked into 'World Turning', and is still part of the band's concerts today. The last part of the set focused on Jeremy Spencer's crowd-pleasing, if undisciplined, Elvis Presley and Little Richard impersonations, along with his own 'Teenage Darling'.

Fleetwood Mac shared the bill at the Fillmore West with American blues guitarist, John Hammond Jr., and The Byrds, at that time successfully transitioning from their *Sweetheart of the Rodeo* period to the earthier McGuinn/Parsons/White/Battin line-up, the most stable and longest-lived of any configuration of The Byrds.

The following week, Fleetwood Mac headlined five nights at the Whisky a Go Go in Los Angeles, supported by The Litter – then on the way down but remembered for their garage band classic 'Action Woman' – and Boz Scaggs, on the way up after the release of his debut album the previous summer.

Midway through their Whisky residency, they taped versions of 'Rattlesnake Shake' and 'Coming Your Way' for TV's *Playboy After Dark*. 'Rattlesnake Shake' – a paean to masturbation – was somehow an appropriate choice and was surely deliberate: 'Now, I know this guy/His name is Mick/Now, he don't care when he ain't got no chick/He do the shake/The rattlesnake shake/And jerks away the blues'.

For the rest of January, Fleetwood Mac worked their way across the continent, from Seattle and Vancouver to Atlanta and New Orleans. Jeremy Spencer's self-titled album – the first solo album by a current member of Fleetwood Mac – was released on 23 January and is an interesting footnote to the Fleetwood Mac discography. All five members of the band took part.

As January turned into February, Fleetwood Mac performed three dates at The Warehouse in New Orleans, playing hour-long sets supporting the Grateful Dead. All three concerts were professionally recorded and are available in collectors' circles in quite wonderful quality stereo sound. The 29 January date has been released as *The Warehouse Tapes*, a grey-market 'radio broadcast' copyright-expired recording.

Fleetwood Mac flew north to Boston to appear for three nights – 5, 6 and 7 February – at the Boston Tea Party: a venue on Lansdowne Street that from 1967 to 1970 hosted many of the classic rock bands. Fleetwood Mac had appeared there in November 1969 (supporting Joe Cocker) and December 1969, and in the weeks before and after their appearances, the Boston Tea Party would present concerts by Taj Mahal, The Who, Santana, Mountain, Humble Pie, The Incredible String Band, The Nice, The Allman Brothers Band, Jethro Tull, Johnny Winter, Grateful Dead, B. B. King, The Byrds, The Kinks, Neil Young and Crazy Horse, Ten Years After, MC5, Family, Stone The Crows, Argent and The Faces.

Fleetwood Mac were supported on this series of dates by the James Gang, featuring 22- year-old Joe Walsh. Delaney & Bonnie and Friends with Eric Clapton would appear there the same week. Both Joe Walsh and Eric Clapton would sit in with Fleetwood Mac on at least one of these dates. All three of Fleetwood Mac's concerts were again recorded, this time for a proposed live album. But the project was shelved after Peter Green's departure from the band, and the tapes remained unreleased until 1985 when seven songs were released on the album *Live in Boston*. A 1998 remixed three-volume CD set titled *Live in Boston: Remastered* collected virtually all of the available tracks from the Boston Tea Party concerts. This amazing album, if proof were needed, verifies the strength of the Green/Kirwan/Spencer/McVie/Fleetwood line-up. These are not mono radio broadcasts, nor reel-to-reel recordings by a guy at the back of the room, but brilliantly-mixed professional multi-tracks that practically fizz with energy.

From their own compositions, Peter Green sings 'Black Magic Woman', 'Rattlesnake Shake' (two versions, both 24 minutes long), a devastating thirteen-minute 'The Green Manalishi (With The Two Prong Crown)', 'Oh Well Part One' and a new song, 'Sandy Mary'.

Danny Kirwan takes the lead on his songs 'Coming Your Way' from *Then Play On*, 'Like it This Way' from the recent *Blues Jam at Chess* album, 'Loving Kind', and his enervating 'Only You'.

Jeremy Spencer does his Elvis, Little Richard, Jerry Lee Lewis and Fabian schtick, and takes on no fewer than seven Elmore James songs: 'I Can't Hold Out', 'Got Yo Move' (two versions), 'Stranger Blues', 'Red Hot Mama', 'Madison Blues', 'The Sun Is Shining' and 'Oh Baby'.

Green sings Anthony 'Duster' Bennett's 'Jumping at Shadows' (two versions) and gives an awesome take on B.B. King's 'If You Let Me Love You'. There's also a quite lovely version of 'World In Harmony', which shows how far Green and Kirwan were moving away from the limitations of the blues they had been playing for the last few years. There are two tedious jams, one of these with added Joe Walsh and Eric Clapton. The set was repackaged in 2013 as simply *Boston*.

Tim Sommer discussed the recordings in *The Observer* in 2015:

> Although these (recordings) showcase Green's stellar blend of economy and ferocity, the real scene-stealer on these recordings are Jeremy Spencer's ecstatic rockabilly covers. These oldies combust a Velvets-like overdrive while also strongly resembling the head-bang-a-billy of the early Flaming Groovies, and they are goddamn hot.

The tour continued to New York for dates at the Fillmore East, with Fleetwood Mac added to a bill with the Grateful Dead and The Allman Brothers Band: Peter Green and most the Allmans joined the Grateful Dead on stage for 'Dark Star' and 'Lovelight'. Two days later, a concert at Madison Square Garden included Sly and the Family Stone, Fleetwood Mac and Grand Funk Railroad: a startlingly diverse but intriguing line-up. The three-month North American tour ended on 15 February 1970 in Worcester, MA, and two weeks later, Fleetwood Mac undertook a short tour of both the Republic of Ireland and Northern Ireland, with dates in Dublin, Cork and Belfast.

Whilst undoubtedly crowd-pleasing, fifty years on, the different facets of Fleetwood Mac's live shows in spring 1970 sit uneasily together: the pure blues retreads, Kirwan's experimentation, Green's melancholia, and

Spencer's exuberating finale. Something had to give, and it was during a tour of Europe that Peter Green – their founder and one of the greatest guitarists of his generation – would leave his own band.

Peter Green's Decline Commences

Fleetwood Mac travelled to Europe for concerts in Paris, Basel, Zurich, Lausanne, Amsterdam, Londerzeel, Rotterdam, Hanover, Berlin, Hamburg and Dusseldorf.

On 22 March 1970, Peter Green took LSD at a party at a commune in Munich. This incident was later cited by the band's manager Clifford Davis as the crucial point in Peter Green's mental decline. Roadie, Dinky Dawson, remembers that Green went to the party with another roadie, Dennis Keane and that when Keane returned to the band's hotel to explain that Green would not leave, Keane, Dawson and Mick Fleetwood travelled there to fetch him.

'We finally found Peter lying in a sunken den that was padded generously with huge cushions and bathed in various psychedelic lights', Dawson wrote in his book *Life on the Road*. 'He was obviously tripping on some very potent LSD, and Mick had to carefully explain to him what was going on. Only after a long negotiation were we able to induce Pete to return with us, but the person we brought back to the hotel would never again be the man I'd known.'

In contrast, speaking in 2009, Green stated that he had fond memories of jamming at the commune: 'I had a good play there, it was great, someone recorded it, they gave me a tape. There were people playing along, a few of us just fooling around and it was ... yeah it was great'. He told Jeremy Spencer at the time, 'That's the most spiritual music I've ever recorded in my life'.

BBC Session: In Concert

The release of *Live at the BBC* by The Beatles in 1994 alerted fans to a so-far untapped wealth of unusual and often unheard live-in-the-studio performances recorded for BBC radio. Over the next few years, archive recordings from the 1960s and early 1970s – by the likes of Curved Air, Dire Straits, ELO, Fairport Convention, Free, Moody Blues, Sandy Denny and Status Quo (an eight-disc box set, no less) – would add colour to the established canon.

Fleetwood Mac recorded fourteen separate BBC radio sessions between November 1967 and October 1969 and another seven in 1970-1971.

At the Paris Theatre on 9 April – recorded for *In Concert* and broadcast ten days later – the band's set opened with 'Rattlesnake Shake', commercially released in 1995 as the opening track on *Live at the BBC*. 'Underway' – one of Peter Green's songs from *Then Play On* – preceded 'Tiger': an up-tempo cover of a rocker first recorded by Fabian, with Jeremy Spencer in full Little Richard mode. A stunning fifteen-minute version of 'The Green Manalishi (With The Two Prong Crown)' is possibly the best version of this classic track: Green and Kirwan are at the peak of their work together. This version has never been officially released. A tough take on 'Stranger Blues' is followed by 'World In Harmony', soon to be recorded as the band's next B-side. The set ends with a lively but non-essential take on 'Great Balls Of Fire' and a bluesy but very ragged 'Twist And Shout'.

Back on the road, Fleetwood Mac headlined the Halifax Pop and Blues Concert at the Thrum Hall rugby league stadium on 11 April, supported by Chicken Shack, The Tremeloes, The Foundations, The Flying Machine and Salt and Pepper (not the 1980s 'Push It' pop duo). The wisdom of holding an outdoor concert in the North of England in April was questionable. Adverse weather conditions meant that only around 3,000 attended, falling well short of the anticipated 35,000. The organisers made a substantial loss of £6,000.

At the Lyceum in London the following evening, Fleetwood Mac were supported by The Idle Race. Vocalist Dave Walker – who would join Fleetwood Mac in 1972 – had replaced Jeff Lynne in the Idle Race in the early weeks of 1970. Walker recalls:

> We were fortunate enough to open for Fleetwood Mac's original line-up at the Lyceum, and they were the most impressive group I had had the privilege of sharing a stage with since The Beatles in 1963. The original line-up was very charismatic, with Green dressed Cossack-like, and the rhythm section of Mick and John, one of the best ever. Kirwan's guitar very classy. Jeremy seemed to balance out very nicely the serious side of the band, although, at the same time, his old-time rock and roll songs were done very diligently and well. Perhaps one of the best bands to be heard.

'The Green Manalishi (With The Two Prong Crown)' b/w 'World In Motion'

UK single release: 15 May 1970 (highest chart position: 10).
US single release: June 1970 (did not chart)

During April, the band taped their final songs with Peter Green. According to Peter Lewry in *The Complete Recording Sessions*, these were recorded at Warner studios in Hollywood on 14 April 1970. If so, they must have flown to the US immediately after their Lyceum concert – taking engineer Martin Birch with them – and returned in time for a Scottish tour the following week.

Martin Birch: 'The weirdest session I've ever taken part in. Peter wasn't communicating very much. The whole atmosphere was very, very strange'.

Rolling Stone: 'The Green Manalishi (With The Two Prong Crown)' is a 'miasmic proto-metal blues freakout... inspired by a dream that Green had while on mescaline, in which he was visited by a green dog that represented money'. Or as Mick Fleetwood would have it, 'a pulsating slab of blues rhythm chords topped with howling solos about the devil, the darkness within, and the alluring temptation of descending into madness'.

It's nothing short of remarkable. Such was the popularity of Fleetwood Mac in the UK at this time that the song was a big hit single – one of the darkest songs to have graced the top ten.

Now, when the day goes to sleep
And the full moon looks
The night is so black that the darkness cooks
Don't you come creepin' around
Makin' me do things I don't wanna do

Peter Green:

I think 'Green Manalishi' was probably the least appreciated song of mine. I had a dream where I woke up and I couldn't move, literally immobile on the bed. I had to fight to get back into my body. I had this message that came to me while I was like this, saying that I was separate from people like shop assistants, and I saw a picture of a female shop assistant and a wad of pound notes, and there was this other message saying, 'You're not what you used to be. You think you're better than them. You used to be an everyday person like a shop assistant, just a regular working person'. I had been separated from it because I had too much money. So I thought, 'How can I change that?'. Making 'Green Manalishi' was one of the best memories. Mixing it down in the studio and listening back to it. I thought it would make number one: Danny and me playing those shrieking guitars together, lots of drums, bass guitars, all kinds of things, six-string basses.

John McVie: 'I didn't really care about the six-string bit. I did think it was a bit weird. I don't know what the thinking was behind it. A bit of ego, maybe? Or a wrap-up to the song? I've no idea. It was great to listen to, as I couldn't have done it'.

'It took me at least two years to recover from that song', Green recalled. 'When I listened to it, there was so much power there, it exhausted me.'

Jeremy Spencer is thought not to have been present at the recording sessions.

The rare B-side – the serene guitar instrumental 'World In Harmony' – is the only Green/Kirwan joint-writing credit. It has a definite Californian feel, and hints of the great music these two men could have made together in the future.

Pop Proms 1970

A short tour of Scotland (Dundee, Aberdeen and Edinburgh) preceded Fleetwood Mac headlining the fifth night of the Pop Proms 1970:a series of concerts at the Roundhouse in London. For 25 shillings each night, fans could attend a remarkable series of concerts of big-name bands, and some less remembered, each hosted by John Peel.

20 April: Traffic, Mott the Hoople, Bronco, If
21 April: T. Rex, Pretty Things, Elton John, Heavy Jelly
22 April: Johnny Winter, Jucy Luicy, Quintessence
23 April: Fairport Convention, Fotheringay, Matthews Southern Comfort
24 April: Fleetwood Mac, Mighty Baby, Hookfoot
25 April: Ginger Baker's Airforce, Toe Fat, Jodi Grind

The entire Fleetwood Mac concert has been bootlegged in excellent quality. Their set that night comprised 'Black Magic Woman', 'Before The Beginning', 'World In Harmony', 'Only You', 'Madison Blues', 'Got to Move', 'The Green Manalishi', 'Merry Go Round', 'Like It This Way', 'Coming Your Way', 'Stranger Blues', 'Tiger', 'Rattlesnake Shake', Underway', 'Albatross', 'Jenny, Jenny' and 'Keep A Knockin'.

As with the Halifax concert earlier in the month, a planned seven-hour concert on Saturday 25 April was rained off. The Spring Thing, at Reading FC, would have seen Fleetwood Mac supported by Chicken Shack, jazz-rockers Colosseum, local blues guitarist Mike Cooper, Viv Stanshall's post-Bonzos Big Grunt, poetry collective The Liverpool Scene, and a solo set by Christine Perfect.

BBC Session: Top Gear

Fleetwood Mac recorded a live session at the Playhouse Theatre in
London on 27 April for John Peel's popular *Top Gear* radio programme.
'Sandy Mary' is a Peter Green original played in concerts at the time. Both
'World In Harmony' and 'Tiger' were recorded once more, along with
'Only You' (the only studio recording of this Danny Kirwan original) and
Green's 'Leaving Town Blues' – first recorded by Fleetwood Mac during
sessions for their debut album in December 1967. 'Sandy Mary' and 'Only
You' from this broadcast are available on *Live at the BBC*.

The Aquae Sulis Incident

Three dates in the England provinces at Manchester, Coventry and Redcar
in early May, preceded Fleetwood Mac's headline appearance at the
The Aquae Sulis Incident: a day-long festival at Bath's football stadium,
Twerton Park, on 23 May 1970. Fleetwood Mac over-ran the curfew, and
the power to the stage was switched off.

This festival was overshadowed by the more famous Bath Festival of
Blues and Progressive Music, held the following month at the Bath and
Wells Showgrounds in Shepton Mallett, which saw Led Zeppelin and Pink
Floyd headline on successive evenings.

Appearing with Fleetwood Mac at this other Bath festival were
Chicken Shack, Juicy Lucy, Sam Apple Pie, Matthews Southern Comfort,
Quintessence, Wildmouth and Wishbone Ash. At that time, Wishbone
Ash had yet to record their debut album – guitarist Andy Powell had seen
Fleetwood Mac at the Windsor Blues Festival and has said that this was his
key inspiration to become a professional musician. Matthews Southern
Comfort were six months away from their biggest hit: a cover of Joni
Mitchell's 'Woodstock'.

Farewell Peter Green

Beginning with the melancholia of 'Man Of The World', Green's
bandmates began to notice changes in his state of mind.

Clifford Davis:

Peter told me privately that he felt it was wrong that a group of
entertainers such as Fleetwood Mac should earn such vast sums of money
when, in fact, other people in the world didn't have enough to eat. He
put it to the band that all profits other than running costs be given to
needy people.

Mick Fleetwood recalls Green becoming concerned about accumulating wealth: 'I had conversations with Peter Green around that time, and he was obsessive about us not making money, wanting us to give it all away. And I'd say, 'Well, you can do it, I don't wanna do that, and that doesn't make me a bad person'.

Green said, in *Fleetwood Mac, The Authorised Biography* (1978):

I wanted to have a charity group, earning no money over the top, and give my money to starving children in Biafra, and things like that. I thought I had too much money to be happy and normal. I felt I didn't deserve it.

Mick Fleetwood: '(It was) a guilt-ridden decision, I think'.

Peter Green fulfilled prior commitments of a recording session for BBC-TV's *Disco 2* (performing 'Tiger', broadcast on 30 May) and a final live performance at the Roundhouse in London on 28 May 1970. Green's departure, says Christine McVie, 'was an out-of-the-blue shock to everybody. Peter had been quite happy and was starting to write this really incredible music like 'Green Manalishi'. It was like he was being lifted'.

'In the span of a few months', recalls Mick Fleetwood, 'he generated from a vibrant, confident man, into a sad and fragile soul. I felt helpless and devastated watching him slip away. Losing Peter was like taking the rudder out of a sailing boat. We were drifting, with no map, and no land in sight'.

Green said in a 1970 interview: 'There are many reasons why I'm leaving; the main thing being that I feel it's time for a change. I want to change my whole life because I don't want to be a part of the conditioned world, and as much as possible, I'm getting out of it'.

Danny Kirwan later said that he was not surprised. 'We just didn't get on too well basically ... We played some good stuff together, we played well together, but we didn't get on'.

Green graciously performed with his former bandmates on *Top of the Pops* on 17 June 1970, lip-syncing to 'The Green Manalishi'. It was his last performance as a full-time member of Fleetwood Mac. He was a member of his own band for fewer than three years.

'It was like taking the underpinnings out of a bridge', John McVie suggests. 'We were quite happily going along and suddenly we were faced by a future without Peter.'

Getting It Together In The Country: Part 1

Peter Green so dominated the British perception of Fleetwood Mac that the band would not regain the popularity that it had with him in their home country for six or seven years. With Green gone, Mick Fleetwood would from now on be the de facto leader of Fleetwood Mac. His first decision echoed Steve Winwood's band Traffic, who had lived together in a house in Berkshire from 1967 to 1969.

'The cottage thing came about for practical reasons really', Winwood reminisces. 'We were staying in a house in London, and whenever we wanted to play, the neighbours would be banging on the walls. We wanted somewhere where we could just play whenever we wanted. We found this cottage in the Berkshire Downs. It was a big estate with a sort of hovel for the gamekeeper, which was what we rented.'

'This period of transition taught me what it means to be in a band', Mick Fleetwood recalled. 'The fragmentation caused by losing Peter was amplified by the fact that none of us lived together. Getting everyone together to rehearse… was a drag. London was full of so many distractions. The only thing that made sense to me, was a move to the country. Fresh air, a change of scene, and a bit of communal living, was what we needed.'

Band members, wives, girlfriends and roadies lived together in a converted oast house near Alton in Hampshire. Mick Fleetwood: 'We lived there for six wonderful months.'
John McVie said later:

The band living together was, in reflection, a great time. Actually, there were two houses. The first was Kiln House. We were there to 'get it together at a house in the country'. It was a beautiful English summer, and I think we only worked the last couple of weeks of a three-month stay. The rest was spent eating, drinking and doing 'illegal substances'. That was when Chris joined. Not for the 'illegal substances', but to fill out the band sound. And she certainly did that.

Christine McVie, speaking to *Mojo* in 2015:

Downstairs were two huge empty rooms, one had a grand piano in it and I used to tinker with it, and Mick would come down and say (whispers) 'You ought to try and write songs, you should write'. I was gently nudged in the back. I started to try because Mick was so encouraging. He'd go, 'Wow, that's great! Let's record it!'. And suddenly we had drums on this thing that

I thought was useless and it was sounding really good. That spurred me on because I believed whatever I wrote, Mick would turn it into something.

Kiln House

Personnel:

Danny Kirwan: guitar, vocals; lead vocals on 'Station Man', 'Jewel-Eyed Judy' and 'Tell Me All The Things You Do'

Mick Fleetwood: drums, percussion

John McVie: bass guitar

Jeremy Spencer: guitar, vocals, piano; lead vocals on 'This Is The Rock', 'Blood On The Floor', 'Hi Ho Silver (Honey Hush)', 'Buddy's Song', 'One Together' and 'Mission Bell'

with

Christine McVie: backing vocals, piano, electric piano

Recorded June–July 1970 at De Lane Lea Studios, London.

Produced by Fleetwood Mac.

Album release: 18 September 1970.

Highest chart placings: UK; 39, US: 69

Side one: 'This Is The Rock', 'Station Man', 'Blood On The Floor', 'Hi Ho Silver (Honey Hush)', 'Jewel-Eyed Judy'

Side two: 'Buddy's Song', 'Earl Gray', 'One Together', 'Tell Me All The Things You Do' 'Mission Bell'

'Jewel-Eyed Judy' b/w 'Station Man'

US single release: January 1971 (did not chart). The single edit of 'Station Man' is on 50 Years – Don't Stop.

Kiln House, recorded in London in June and July 1970, is an album of two contrasting halves: almost two bands with the same players. Six of the songs feature Jeremy Spencer's rock-and-roll and country pastiches. 'This Is The Rock' channels the country-blues of Elvis Presley and the Jordanaires. Spencer and Kirwan work well together here and the backing vocals are great, but even at fewer than three minutes in length, it seems overlong. 'Blood On The Floor' is a 6/8 country-and-western ballad, very tongue-in-cheek and lots of fun, if totally out of place on a Fleetwood Mac album. 'Honey Hush' (listed as 'Hi Ho Silver') is a roof-raising take on a Big Joe Turner classic, with a very good slide guitar solo. 'Buddy's Song' is a very obvious Buddy Holly tribute, with many of Holly's famous song titles spread through the lyric and Mick Fleetwood copying Jerry Allison's trademark tom tom runs. It becomes tedious after about sixty seconds. 'Mission Bell' starts beautifully but 'squanders a lovely opening when (Jeremy) Spencer starts singing', according to Rikky Rooksby. 'It could be Billy Fury with sentimental production.'

Spencer comes out from behind his Elmore James/Elvis Presley/Buddy Holly masks for his most successful contribution to the album: 'One Together', a heartfelt country song apparently written for his wife. There is a delicate slide guitar solo and block harmony backing vocals that could be straight from *Rumours*.

Whilst Jeremy Spencer's songs for *Kiln House* lack a strong original vision, Danny Kirwan comes into his own as a writer, singer and guitar player. 'Earl Gray' is a gorgeous, reverb-laden guitar exploration, with some decorous piano changes. An early version of 'Earl Gray' – titled 'Farewell' – was later released on the compilation, *The Vaudeville Years*. 'Jewel-Eyed Judy' – co-credited to Kirwan with Mick Fleetwood and John McVie – is a dreamy Beatlesque ballad with echoes of Badfinger and Big Star. It was written for the band's friend, Judy Wong – their manager's PA and secretary – who worked for them behind the scenes for many years. Shimmering Wurlitzer piano and languid guitars underpin a fragile three-chord arrangement that explodes with real dynamism in the chorus. A terrific song.

'Station Man' and 'Tell Me All Things You Do' are out-and-out classics. 'Station Man' – co-written by Kirwan with Jeremy Spencer and John McVie – pushes Fleetwood Mac further from their pure blues roots. It's a beautifully arranged song, full of dynamics, fading in from silence with block harmonies (Christine McVie's voice is very evident) and a strong, confident vocal from Danny Kirwan. There are also two wonderful guitar solos: the second is just getting going when the song fades. The rest of the band liked 'Station Man' so much it remained in their set for several years after Kirwan left, right through to the Buckingham and Nicks era. The Who's Pete Townshend has admitted that he 'borrowed' the riff to 'Station Man' and used it in 'Won't Get Fooled Again', recorded in 1971. 'Tell Me All Things You Do' is a twisted boogie with swirling electric piano and snorting guitars. It fades too soon after four minutes. The song often opened the band's set in 1972 and was rehearsed in February 1977 with Lindsey Buckingham's wah-wah guitar leads. Remarkably, 'Tell Me All The Things You Do' returned to Fleetwood Mac's set in 2018, sung by Christine McVie and Neil Finn.

Mick Fleetwood later said of the *Kiln House* period: 'Danny came to the fore more than anybody when it came to the songwriting, and showed his great melodic style'.

Kiln House would be the last Fleetwood Mac album to make the UK charts for five years. In contrast, it was their first album to break into the top 100 in the US, reaching number 69. The band's star would steadily rise there through relentless touring. *Melody Maker* in 1971 said:

> In progressing from a raw 'blues revival' band, Fleetwood Mac have gone forward in terms of production and performance and backwards in their search for material and style... Not a creative album, but entertaining and well-played.

'I think *Kiln House* was a pretty good album', says Jeremy Spencer. 'The introduction of Christine Perfect was a good and necessary asset. I also had been listening to country music and I wanted to get more into vocals, and I was enjoying the fact that we could do harmonies.'

Robert Christgau said in *Village Voice in* 1970:

> Despite the departure of the miraculously fluent Peter Green, the mansions in their jazzy blues/rock and roll guitar heaven are spacier than ever. A country parody called 'Blood on the Floor' is less charitable than one would hope, but it's more than balanced off by Jeremy Spencer's membership pledge to the rockabilly auxiliary: 'This Is the Rock'. And somebody up there loves Buddy Holly so much, he unearthed 'Buddy's Song' by Buddy's mother.

Tim Sommer commented in *The Observer* in 2015:

> Although Fleetwood Mac's first Green-less album, *Kiln House* (1970), is a relatively unsatisfying transitional album (the group is, unknowingly, searching for a bridge between the old blues Mac and the more melodically-driven band to come), it features Kirwan's gentle, persuasive, almost Harrison-esque instrumental 'Earl Grey', which sounds like a slightly wet REM trying to play Cream's 'Badge' (that's a compliment).

Clifford Davis Releases a Single

One of the rarest Fleetwood Mac-related releases comes from mid-1970. Manager Clifford Davis released a single on Reprise in the UK on 17 July. His self-written 'Come On Down And Follow Me' was backed with a version of 'Homework': the Otis Rush song that Fleetwood Mac played in concert in 1969-1970.

It's entirely possible that one or more members of Fleetwood Mac play on these songs: it certainly *sounds* like Peter Green's guitar playing on 'Homework', and, rumour has it, that Green plays all of the instruments on 'Come On Down And Follow Me'. It seems likely that these songs were recorded during sessions for Peter Green's first solo album, *The End of the Game*.

This followed a release the previous October of new versions of the Fleetwood Mac songs 'Before The Beginning' and 'Man Of The World'. These are Fleetwood Mac's original instrumental tracks remixed, with the addition of a delicious string arrangement and a new Davis vocal.

BBC Radio Session: First Gear

A recording session at Maida Vale Studio Four, London, for BBC Radio's *First Gear*, dates from 7 July 1970. The four-piece band performed a 1950s-throwback set comprising 'Buddy's Song' from *Kiln House*, The Everly Brothers' 'When Will I Be Loved', Jeremy Spencer's solo track 'Jenny Lee', Danny Kirwan's otherwise unknown gentle rock and roll song 'When I See My Baby', and Big Joe Turner's 'Honey Hush', also recorded for *Kiln House*. Broadcast on 22 July 1970, all five songs are on *Live at the BBC*. Here is the sound of a band having no idea what to do next. Salvation was close at hand.

Christine McVie Joins Fleetwood Mac

Christine McVie had left Chicken Shack in August 1969, preferring to spend time with her husband. Chicken Shack's version of Etta James' 'I Would Rather Go Blind' had been a top 20 hit in June and July 1969, and McVie was voted 'best female vocalist' in the 1969 *Melody Maker* pop poll. Mike Vernon urged her to make an album. She recorded this over the next several months and toured with her own band as 1969 turned into 1970. The album, *Christine Perfect* (she didn't change her name until later in the year), includes a version of Danny Kirwan's 'When You Say' from *Then Play On,* which included guitar by Kirwan and bass from Christine's husband, John.

Tim Sommer in *The Observer* (2015) describes 'When You Say' as, 'a positively Robert Wyatt-ish song of childlike simplicity and deep sentiment'; and McVie's version as 'extraordinary, far more reminiscent of the string-driven autumn simplicity of Nico's 'Chelsea Girl' than anything the Mac (in any configuration) ever recorded. Find this recording, and stick it on your Fleetwood Mac mixtape, in a place of honour'.

Following her success as a member of Fleetwood Mac, the album was reissued in 1976 under the name *The Legendary Christine Perfect Album*.

Christine's recruitment to Fleetwood Mac added three important components to their sound: her soulful voice – which ripened and deepened during the 1970s – her skills as a songwriter and, crucially, her electric-piano-playing, which added an important new dimension to the Fleetwood/McVie rhythm section, tying the bass and drums together. Christine McVie: I've never considered myself a lead keyboard player... but as part of the rhythm section.

As much as any other factor, the foundations of Fleetwood Mac's huge success after 1975 was due to these three elements coming together in 1970.

In August 1970, Fleetwood Mac flew to the US for live dates in Detroit, San Francisco, Vancouver, Los Angeles, New York and Lambertville.

'John and the band were working up a new album and a new stage act', Christine McVie told writer and rock genealogist Pete Frame:

They were down to a four-piece, and just before the start of a tour, they suddenly felt like they needed another instrument to fill out the sound. And there I was, sitting around doing next to nothing and knowing all the songs back to front because I'd been watching them rehearse for the past three months.

A typical setlist for these dates, in this case from the Fillmore East on 28 August, was 'Crazy About You (Can't Hold Out Much Longer)' (from Christine's solo album), 'Can't Stop Loving My Baby' (an Elmore James cover), 'Mission Bell' and 'Tell Me All The Things You Do (both from *Kiln House*), 'Get Like You Used To Be' and 'I'd Rather Go Blind (both carried over from Chicken Shack), 'Station Man' (from *Kiln House*), 'Dust My Blues' (the perennial Robert Johnson song), 'Blue Suede Shoes' (viz Carl Perkins), Jeremy Spencer's 'Teenage Darling' and a cover of Chris Montez' 'Let's Dance'.

Getting it Together in the Country: Part 2

Just before leaving for America, the band bought a secluded Victorian mansion in Headley, Hampshire, eight miles east of Kiln House. Led Zeppelin lived and worked at a house in the same village: Headley Grange.

Benifold (or Benifols, or Benifolds, as some would have it) was bought jointly by Fleetwood Mac and their manager Clifford Davis for £23,000. The previous owners had been members of a monastic order. John McVie:

> There were so many good times there. Having our parents down for the day on a weekend, going down the local, Chris's great Sunday dinners, oh, and a bit of music. The worst: getting busted. Having to deal with Jenny's dead rabbits, who'd stiffed out in the cold at Christmas... going through all the legal stuff when our ex-manager, Davis, put a 'fake' Mac on tour.

Mick and his wife Jenny Boyd lived in the servants' quarters. John and Christine McVie lived in a separate wing with their own kitchen and living-room: it was at Chris's kitchen table that all-important Fleetwood Mac business was discussed.

Radio 1 Club and Sounds of the Seventies

Fleetwood Mac recorded two sessions for BBC radio in November 1970. The first was for the *Radio 1 Club*: a lunchtime show broadcast from different locations around the UK. The band recorded five songs at the BBC's Paris Theatre in London on 10 November, and these were broadcast on 14 and 16 December 1970: Chris McVie belting out a swampy version of Little Walter's 'Crazy About You (Can't Hold Out Much Longer)', recorded for her solo album and the opening number of their most recent tour; Peter Green's 'Sandy Mary'; Danny Kirwan's 'Down At The Crown For Now' – a song about the pub along the lane from the band's house at Benifold; another of Jeremy Spencer's Fabian impressions, Pomus and Shuman's 'Turn Me Loose'; and a robust rendition of the classic 'Tell Me All The Things You Do' from *Kiln House*.

Two weeks later, they recorded 'Down At The Crown For Now', 'Purple Dancer' (the B-side of their next single) and 'Station Man' from *Kiln House*, at Maida Vale Studio Five, London, for *Mike Harding – Sounds of the Seventies* (not the folk singer/comedian). These were broadcast on 1 December 1970. Five of the songs from these two sessions were released in 2003 on the album, *Madison Blues*.

'Dragonfly' b/w 'The Purple Dancer'
UK single release: March 1971 (did not chart)

The departure of Peter Green pushed Danny Kirwan to write more songs. And although the pressure of these demands would force him out of the band in 1972, his contributions to the next two Fleetwood Mac albums were significant. The last stand-alone Fleetwood Mac single, Kirwan's dreamy 'Dragonfly' is embellished by some of the most delicate, exquisite guitar parts in the Fleetwood Mac canon. The lyrics to 'Dragonfly' were adapted from W. H. Davies' 1927 poem of the same name.

Now, when my roses are half buds, half flowers,
And loveliest, the king of flies has come-
It was a fleeting visit, all too brief;
In three short minutes he has seen them all,
And rested, too, upon an apple tree.

There, his round shoulders humped with emeralds,
A gorgeous opal crown set on his head,
And all those shining honours to his breast-
'My garden is a lovely place' thought I,
'But is it worthy of such a guest?'

'Like many of the band's songs dominated by Kirwan', writes Richie Unterberger, '('Dragonfly') was an easy-going, wistful number with flowing, almost jazzy guitar, this time enhanced by Christine McVie's vocal harmonies'.

In his book, *The Complete Guide to the Music of Fleetwood Mac*, Rikky Rooksby stated: ' ... wonderfully textured guitar-playing. It has shimmering chords and the tune coming down in octaves ... This is far and away the best thing which Kirwan ever wrote'.

For years, the song was only available as a 7' single and on the 1971 *Greatest Hits*. More recently it has been included on *The Best of Peter Green's Fleetwood Mac* (2002) and on the *1969 to 1974* box set released in 2020.

For the next five years, Fleetwood Mac would have no hit singles – other than a re-release of 'Albratross' in 1973 – and no major hit albums.

A short UK tour saw out their responsibilities for 1970. It had been an eventful year.

1971

Sounds of the Seventies

Fleetwood Mac's next session for the BBC was recorded on 5 January 1971 at Maida Vale Studio Four in London. They recorded five songs: 'Start Again': an early version of 'Morning Rain' from *Future Games*; 'Teenage Darling' from Jeremy Spencer's solo album; a scintillating acoustic take of Son House's 'Preachin''; Christine McVie singing Chicken Shack's 'Get Like You Used To Be'; and the band's forthcoming single, Danny Kirwan's 'Dragonfly'. Four of these songs were broadcast on *Mike Harding – Sounds of the Seventies* on 23 January. 'Dragonfly' was held back until 27 March to coincide with its release as a single. 'Preachin'' has been released on *Live at the BBC*.

Goodbye Jeremy Spencer

Fleetwood Mac travelled to North America once again in February 1971. Live recordings from the tour were released many years later on *Madison Blues*. This enjoyable and eclectic album includes 'Madison Blues' (another Elmore James cover); 'The Purple Dancer' (the B-side of their most recent single); Kirwan's 'Open The Door'; Son House's 'Preachin''; Robert Johnson's 'Dust My Blues'; Chicken Shack's 'Get Like You Used To Be'; Spencer's 'Don't Go Please Stay' and 'Teenage Darling'; 'Station Man' and 'Honey Hush' from *Kiln House*; 'I'm On My Way' from *Christine Perfect*; and a cover of 'Jailhouse Rock'.

While on tour in February 1971, Jeremy Spencer said he was going out to 'get some groceries', but never returned. After several days of frantic searching, 'we received an anonymous tip. We'd find Jeremy at the Children of God's warehouse in downtown L.A.', Mick Fleetwood says. 'He was staying there under an assumed name.'

'After about two hours of negotiating', says Clifford Davis, 'he walked out (to meet us). His head was shaved; he had changed his name. I asked him if he was there of his own free will. He said, "Yes, I feel at home here, Clifford"'.

'He had been completely brainwashed', insists Mick Fleetwood. 'He was like a child, starstruck. Jeremy Spencer was gone.'

John McVie:

I was sitting next to him on the plane down from San Francisco to L.A., where we had some gigs at the Whisky A Go Go. He was looking out of the window, and then he turned to me and said, 'Why do I have to be here if I don't want to be here?'. Well, everyone in the band had felt like that at one time or another, so I didn't give it a second thought ... but that was the last time I spoke to him for two years.

'I was so dissatisfied with life and myself and everything', Spencer said thirty years later. 'My mind was going nuts. I just needed to make that clean break, to get away.'

Spencer's last live performance with Fleetwood Mac was at the Fillmore West in San Francisco in the second week of February 1971. The four dates at the Whisky A Go Go were cancelled as the band decided what to do next. Contracted to a lengthy American tour, they performed as a four-piece for the next month, with dates in Los Angeles and up and down the east coast to New York (at the soon-to-close Fillmore East), North Carolina, Florida, Maryland, Missouri and Ohio, through to mid-March.

'We had six weeks of the tour left', says Mick Fleetwood. 'The revenue we'd lose cancelling those dates would cost us our house, Benifold, and probably the band. We were at a loss what to do.'

Peter Green Returns

Mick Fleetwood: 'Out of desperation, we reached out to Peter Green'.

Green flew to California to complete the tour. He brought his friend, Nigel Watson, who played the congas on these dates. Twenty-five years later, Green and Watson collaborated again to form the Peter Green Splinter Group.

'When Jeremy 'left' in L.A.', John McVie recalled 35 years later, 'we called Peter, or rather Mick called Peter, to help us finish the tour. Bless his heart; he came straight out. I think we did a couple of 'structured' songs, but to the best of my recollection, we just jammed for two or three hours. It just shows you the strength of Peter's playing at that time, that he could carry that. What a player!'.

Green's first date was on 24 March at the Swing Auditorium in San Bernadino, with two more dates at the Rock Pile, Island Park, Long Island, on the way back to the UK. Mick Fleetwood, in 2014:

He agreed to play 'Black Magic Woman', at whatever point in the set he felt inspired to do so, after which we would do 90 minutes of free-form jamming. This made for an interesting six weeks because not once did we take to the stage knowing what the set would be. Peter never once engaged with the audience … yet at times his playing was so beautiful that it raised goose flesh on my arms. These moments made it all the sadder. This was the long goodbye.

Peter Green's return was always going to be temporary. Jeremy Spencer's permanent replacement would take Fleetwood Mac further from the blues and more towards a slicker, West Coast sound. His name: Bob Welch.

Enter Bob Welch
Mick Fleetwood often acted on instinct.

'Every move that's ever been made', he once admitted, 'was one where I said, 'Don't worry, it will happen. And, touch wood, it has happened. It's like a little magic guiding star'.

When this instinct was right – think of the recruitment of Bob Welch, Bob Weston, Lindsey Buckingham and Stevie Nicks – his band was immeasurably improved, or at least sustained. When it wasn't – Dave Walker, Dave Mason and Bekka Bramlett, as examples – the opposite often applied.

Bob Welch was born in Los Angeles in 1945, the son of a successful Hollywood movie producer. He was the first American recruit to a band that had been, thus far, 100% British.

'I grew up in a showbiz environment', Bob Welch told the *Daily Tennessean* in 2003. 'Jonathan Winters would come to the house. Yul Brynner lived across the street.'

After graduation from high school, Welch moved to Paris for a while, paying his dues backing expat American jazzmen.

'I mostly smoked hash with bearded guys five years older', he told *People* in 1979.

Welch returned to Los Angeles in 1964, still a teenager, and joined The Seven Souls.

The Seven Souls released a single in 1967. Welch formed Head West in 1969 with former members of The Seven Souls. Welch had returned to Paris when he received a call from Mick Fleetwood asking him to join Fleetwood Mac. Judy Wong – the band's friend and part-time secretary – was a former high school friend of Welch and had recommended him.

'I said, 'I'll be there in two seconds', he recalled later. ''Could you send me plane fare?' I knew I was being scrutinized, not so much for my musical talents but for my psychological soundness. I just wanted to play guitar in a good band. I wanted to make the music I love. I wanted to travel the world and have adventures.'

Christine McVie, in 1977:

Before we met Bob, we tried a series of really embarrassing auditions, with would-be Eric Claptons coming down to the house. But we just couldn't be so professional about it – y'know. 'What are your credentials?' and all that. It was very difficult for us to say 'Let's try a twelve-bar in D' and listen to some guy wailing away. We'd say goodbye to these guys and realise that we just couldn't do it.

Mick Fleetwood: 'We tried out a few others, but Bob was perfect fit'.

'Bob never actually played a note', Christine McVie says. 'All we did was sit around and talk until dawn, and we just thought he was an incredible person. I remember saying to Mick that I didn't even care what his playing was like; he was such a good person.'

Bob Welch recalled many years later:

The atmosphere when I joined was… different, to say the least. They had just lost their main frontman, Pete Green and Jeremy Spencer, within a year and a half. Everybody was sitting around, smoking a lot of hash, and sort of brooding about Spencer's recent departure, which had been fairly dramatic. Mick and I immediately got along great. He was always the main person that I hung with in Fleetwood Mac. Frankly, I didn't understand Danny Kirwan at all. He made me very nervous and uncomfortable… not meaning to, I suppose, he just did. John and Chris were married at the time, and I mostly saw them together, as a couple, in Chris's upstairs kitchen at Benifold. Chris had a great, sarcastic sense of humour. The atmosphere was, how to say it, emotionally confining. I had just come from working in a band of American guys, Head West, who were all 'high-five' and 'gimme some skin', and 'one-for-all and all-for-one'. By contrast, the Fleetwood Mac'ers seemed, well, 'constipated' and uptight. Also, it was not the type of music that I was used to playing, and, as a newbie, I wanted to do what they expected of me. But they never flat out came out and told me what they wanted because they didn't know. They only knew what they didn't want, which I would have to guess at. People often forget that Fleetwood Mac were very popular in Europe before they were at all known in the US. My concern at the time was more how I could fill Pete Green and Jeremy Spencer's shoes, or more exactly, was I expected to fill them? When I joined, there was a lot of publicity in England, where they had been pretty big 'stars'. Because they had lost their main creative force, Pete Green, the concern was not so much 'how to stay famous', but 'is there a musical reason for this band to continue to exist?'.

Bob Welch, crucially, was Californian: the first American of many to join Fleetwood Mac. His fluid guitar-playing and impressive invention as a musician came with a rather nasal singing voice and a sometimes over-earnest style of lyric writing. But his presence in the band drove the Anglo-American sound that the band developed between 1971 and 1974. It was only when asked to be simultaneously a lead songwriter, lead guitarist, frontman, co-manager and plaintiff, that he would burn out and resign. Meanwhile, Welch moved into Benifold, as he later recalled:

Benifold was a big, three-story, rambling twenty-room house, forty miles south of London in the county of Hampshire. The house had been used as a 'religious retreat' for a long time, and it had two kitchens. Mick and Jenny had their separate quarters, John and Chris theirs. Danny had his on the third floor. Downstairs, there was a studio, partially finished, and a rehearsal room where we rehearsed at any time of day or night. It was really kind of communal living, but I think it helped keep the band together during that time. We couldn't get away from each other! The first year I stayed there, Mick and John – who both owned the house – hadn't yet put in central heating. It was miserable in winter! I'd have to run to the bathtub real fast and turn on the hot water, and then run back to bed until it filled up, and then run back and jump in. It was so cold, like maybe 20 degrees, that the whole bathroom would steam up so much that you couldn't see where the walls were ...

Fleetwood Mac started to work up a new live set and write new songs. For the next year and a half, over two excellent albums, Fleetwood Mac would have the formidable three-vocalist/songwriter line-up of Danny Kirwan, Christine McVie and Bob Welch. The male/female dynamic combined three key elements: Christine McVie's simple, direct songs about the joys and drawbacks of love, Kirwan's coming of age as an effortlessly melodic songwriter, and Welch's merging of his formidable musicianship with a more sideways looks at life.

Bob Welch:

Danny was one of the first people I knew, beside myself, who would try to make pretty elaborate demos of his stuff. He had a Revox tape recorder that, by 'bouncing', he used to be able to get six or eight tracks out of. That still didn't mean that a song stayed the same once the band started learning it. Fleetwood Mac never learned anything verbatim off of a demo. Most often, and in the case of me and Christine's stuff, songs were partially worked out, and then all the band members, in rehearsal, contributed equally to the finished arrangement. Fleetwood Mac was definitely not Danny's band when I joined, which actually made things more stressful for me, as I had assumed there'd be a 'bandleader' that would tell me exactly what they wanted. But there wasn't.

Pinkpop and UK Tour

After rehearsing at Benifold for a few weeks, Bob Welch's first concert appearance with Fleetwood Mac was on 31 May 1971 at the second Pinkpop Festival in Geleen, near Maastricht in the Netherlands. Out went the Elvis and Little Richard covers, in came the more thoughtful, slightly jazzier Bob Welch songs. Some shaky but fascinating film footage exists from the band's performance here. Most of the other acts on the bill were Dutch – Brainbox, a rock band founded by Jan Akkerman (who had left the band eighteen months previously); Focus (Akkerman's current band); folkies CCC Inc; proggers Supersister; and psychedelic band, Shocking Blue, of 'Venus' fame. Other than Fleetwood Mac, the only non-Dutch band were ex-Spencer Davis Band duo Hardin and York.

In June and July 1971, Fleetwood Mac toured the UK in an eight-week slog around small venues, re-establishing their audience and road-testing their new songs. They visited some of the lesser-known outposts of the UK circuit, including the Imperial Hall, Nelson, Lancashire; Nottingham Rowing Club; the Glen Club, Llanelli; the Belfry Hotel, Sutton Coldfield; Felixstowe Pier Pavillion; Southport Floral Hall; Torquay Town Hall; Penzance Winter Gardens and the Orchid Ballroom, Purley.

Between dates, sessions for a new album progressed. The band's next album, *Future Games*, was recorded intermittently at Advision Studios in London between June and August.

Future Games

Personnel:
Danny Kirwan: guitar, vocals
Mick Fleetwood: drums, percussion
Christine McVie: keyboards, vocals
John McVie: bass guitar

Bob Welch: guitar, vocals
with
John Perfect: saxophone on 'What A Shame', harmonica on 'Lay It All Down'
Recorded June–August 1971 at Advision Studios, London.
Produced by Fleetwood Mac.
Album release: 3 September 1971.
Highest chart placings: did not chart UK: did not chart US: 91
Side one: 'Woman Of 1000 Years', 'Morning Rain', 'What A Shame', 'Future Games'
Side two: 'Sands Of Time', 'Sometimes', 'Lay It All Down', 'Show Me A Smile'

'Sands Of Time' b/w 'Lay It All Down'
US Single release: 1971 (did not chart). The single edit of 'Sands Of Time' is on 50 Years – Don't Stop.

Inevitably, *Future Games* is a transitional album: with the Bob Welch/ Danny Kirwan line-up finding its feet. Despite this, or perhaps because of it, *Future Games* is mostly very good. Bob Welch and Christine McVie start to explore the sounds that would finally crack the band in the US, and Danny Kirwan provides three brilliant songs. Nearly all traces of the barrelhousing blues of the Peter Green/Jeremy Spencer band have been excised. And yet, the band didn't have a strong identity, and the record-buying public didn't know what to make of this second post-Green album. It was their first album to miss the UK charts and just crept into the US top 100.

The opening 'Woman Of 1000 Years' sounds like early acoustic Pink Floyd. Both 'Cymbaline' from 1969's *More* and 'A Pillow of Winds' from *Meddle* – the latter recorded concurrently with *Future Games* and released about six weeks after – have a very similar feel with dreamy acoustic guitars, echoey harmony vocals and no drums (but claves and bongos).

'Danny was a very intuitive musician', Bob Welch said. 'He played with a surprising maturity and soulfulness. There was an idealistic and pure thing about him that was great. I think 'Woman Of 1000 Years' was Danny at his best.'

'Woman of 1000 Years' floated on a shining sea of languid, echo-laden acoustic and electric guitars, capped by Kirwan's plaintive vocal and inimitable melodic sense.
(Samuel Graham, *Fleetwood Mac, the Authorised History*, 1978)

'Woman Of 1000 Years' showed an almost Beach Boys-like West Coast rock influence, especially in the newly resonant male/female vocal harmonies, that had largely been absent from previous Fleetwood Mac discs.
(Richie Unterberger, *Fleetwood Mac: The Complete Illustrated History*, 2016)

The gentle 'Sometimes' is Danny Kirwan's take on the gentle country styles of the Grateful Dead and CSNY, with hints of Badfinger and 'Octopus's Garden'. Kirwan's lead vocal is one of his best, full of emotion, and he adds a stinging guitar solo, with amazing left hand vibrato. The song is perhaps two minutes too long. It's a surprise that an edited 'Sometimes' was not picked as the album's single instead of 'Sands Of Time', which was seen perhaps as a more 'group' effort with prominent electric piano, a double-time central section and harmony guitars straight from a Wishbone Ash album.

That he was still only 21 says much about Danny Kirwan's precocity and also of the pressures placed on him: pressures that would force him out of the band the following year.

New boy Bob Welch contributed two songs: 'Future Games' and 'Lay It All Down'. The eight-minute 'Future Games' is a good example of West Coast prog rock with a British twist. The change from a minor to a major key in the chorus, reinforced by some glorious gospel organ, provides a wonderful uplift. The song builds to a climax via striking guitars from both Welch and Kirwan and ebbing harmonies. The lyrics, however, are overwritten:

How many people sit home at night
Wondering if they will be here tonight
Wondering if children will he bring to the light
Inherit the world, or inherit the night
Wondering if neighbours are thinking the same
All of the wild things tomorrow will tame
Talking of journeys that happen in vain

Bob Welch in 1999:

'Future Games' was the first song I did with Fleetwood Mac, and also the title of the album ... which I didn't at all expect. I was thrilled! When I wrote 'Future Games', the Vietnam war was still going strong; they had had the riots in Chicago at the Democratic Convention two years before, Nixon was in the White House, paranoia was in the air. Timothy Leary was hiding from the government in North Africa or somewhere. They were trying to put Larry Flint in jail, they were giving people 80-year jail sentences in Texas for possession of one marijuana joint, and the FBI was wiretapping your grandmother. And I'm only half kidding. The future looked a little grimy, and I wrote 'Future Games' trying to capture that pretty insecure mood I was in.

'Lay It All Down' is a wordy rocker with a twisting guitar riff, a long guitar solo and a heavily-reverbed lead vocal. Christine McVie's brother, John Perfect, guests on harmonica. A slightly faster alternative take was released in November 1992 on *The Chain – 25 Years*, and again in September 2020 on *1969 to 1974*.

Christine McVie's own two songs – 'Morning Rain' and 'Show Me A Smile' – spotlight her maturing songwriting style. The seeds of the band's later commercial success can be clearly heard, especially on 'Morning Rain' which, with its male/female vocal chorus harmonies, could easily be an outtake from *Rumours*. Guitarists Kirwan and Welch bond well on this driving rocker. There is an early version of 'Morning Rain' with the title 'Start Again' on a BBC session recorded on 5 January 1971, prior to Jeremy Spencer's departure. 'Show Me A Smile' is a soothing ballad with a Green-esque counterpoint guitar melody.

Future Games, then, saw Fleetwood Mac moving closer to the melodic pop sound that would finally break them in America. After the band presented the album to their record company, they were told that seven songs were not enough. The funky yet inconsequential, 140 seconds-long 'What A Shame' was hastily recorded as an eighth. A longer take – with Kirwan's and Welch's vocals – can be heard on the *1969 to 1974* box set. It's pretty good.

''What A Shame' was a big jam', Bob Welch said. 'Christine's brother John Perfect played sax.'

David Fricke wrote in 2012:
Future Games (was) dominated by Kirwan's haunted ballads and instrumental facility, with Christine sweetening the suspense with the R&B-flavoured romanticism of her straightforward love songs. Welch, in turn, brought an L.A. polish and smart-pop delicacy that bloomed in his quietly epic title song and his misty-treble guitar interplay with Kirwan, especially on 'Woman Of A Thousand Years'.

The British music weekly, *Sounds*, was complimentary, if not effusive: 'There may not be the very high streaks of fire that Green came up with during his time with them, but the feeling now is one of great warmth, of great purpose'.

Rolling Stone, however, was much harsher.

While Fleetwood Mac was often very good ... with (Peter) Green's departure, they had suffered a discomforting loss of intensity. Last year, while on tour in California, Jeremy Spencer quit, defecting to one of the many strange religious cults so popular in Southern California. Spencer's place was filled, more or less, by American singer-guitarist Bob Welch. So, it is with a lineup of Kirwan, McVie, Welch, Fleetwood, and McVie that Fleetwood Mac is heard on Future Games. For my taste, the album has little to commend. Danny Kirwan is out front on most of the cuts, and sadly his singing and playing appear to have lost their edge. His voice drones, innocuously, he plays almost aimlessly, and the songs he writes are just too long. One of them, 'Sometimes', might have been good, but it lingers on purposelessly and painfully for six and a half minutes. Christine McVie puts in far and away the best performance of the album, but this too is disappointing in the light of her past achievements and potential. Her voice sounds surprisingly weak and emotionless here. Her piano-playing too, is not up to her known capabilities. Still, one of her songs, 'Morning Rain', does have its moments. While Fleetwood and McVie handle their rhythm chores competently, they have usually been heard to be much better. As for Bob Welch, his talent appears to be notable only in its lack of distinction, but perhaps he too has the ability to do better. Future Games is a thoroughly unsatisfactory album. It is thin and anaemic-sounding and I get the impression that no one involved really put very much into it. If Fleetwood Mac have tried to make the transition from an energetic rocking British blues band to a softer, more 'contemporary' rock group, they have failed. If they have simply lost interest, I hope they regain it in time to salvage what was once a very promising band.

Fleetwood Mac had recorded a brilliant album, but no one was listening. It set the pattern followed by the band's next four albums: solid but unspectacular sales in the US, and an almost complete lack of interest in the UK. In 2000, *Future Games* – almost forty years after its release – was certified gold by the Recording Industry Association of America (RIAA) with sales of over half a million copies in the United States.

Final BBC Session and Beat Club

Midway through this busy period, the new-look Fleetwood Mac recorded their final BBC radio session for *Alan Black – Sounds of the Seventies*. The session dates from 1 July 1971 at Aeolian Hall Studio 2, London (broadcast three weeks later) and features three new songs from the in-progress album: Danny Kirwan's 'Woman Of A Thousand Years', Chris McVie's 'Show Me A Smile', and Bob Welch's 'Future Games'.

Later in the month, they performed very tight performances of 'Dragonfly' and 'Lay It All Down' for the German TV series, *The Beat Club*. An outtake titled 'Danny E Minor', might be an early version of 'Danny's Chant' from *Bare Trees*.

On 24 July, Fleetwood Mac headlined a one-day outdoor festival at Small Heath Park in Birmingham. They were supported by Status Quo, who were promoting their third album *Ma Kelly's Greasy Spoon*, which included a cover of Peter Green's 'Lazy Poker Blues' from Fleetwood Mac's *Mr Wonderful*. The tour ended at the Memorial Hall Theatre, in Barry, South Wales, on 31 July 1971. A few days later, Fleetwood Mac flew to the US for two weeks, their sixth visit in twenty months.

Festivals in Germany and Austria

Over Saturday and Sunday, 4 and 5 September 1971, Fleetwood Mac took park in two-day twin Festivals in Speyer, Germany and Vienna, Austria.

On 4 September, the British Rock Meeting, in Speyer, featured Black Sabbath, Curved Air, East Of Eden, Fleetwood Mac, Gentle Giant and Hardin and York; and the British Superstar Meeting in Vienna included performances by Deep Purple, The Faces, Family, Osibisa and Rory Gallagher. The bands swapped venues for the Sunday concerts.

Back to America

Fleetwood Mac returned to the Rock Pile, Long Island, in October 1971, and spent much of the next eleven months on tour in the US (October-November 1971), the UK (December 1971-January 1972), and two further visits to the US (February-May and August 1972).

An early highlight included a date supporting Frank Zappa in Milwaukee on 20 October 1971.

From September 1971 to May 1973, Fleetwood Mac would support Deep Purple at over sixty concerts in the US. Bob Welch said later:

Deep Purple was not a very friendly band to tour with, as I recall. Or more precisely, John Lord, Roger Glover and Ian Paice were alright guys, but Ian Gillian and Ritchie Blackmore were totally pretty prima-donna-ish. Ian Gillian stayed in a separate hotel from the rest of Deep Purple, and he'd arrive every night in his own limo, which would drive right up to the stage just as the band was going on. He did the show and then left. Never talked to anybody. They obviously were not all getting along. Blackmore had his own dressing room, which nobody could enter, and he never talked to anybody either. We'd sometimes see John Lord or Glover or Paice at breakfast or in the hotel lobby. They were pretty nice guys.

Fleetwood Mac's setlist at the Whisky A Go Go in West Hollywood, on 22 November 1971 – a recording of which circulates amongst collectors – was typical of this tour: 'Tell Me All The Things You Do', 'Future Games', 'Morning Rain', 'I'd Rather Go Blind', 'Trinity', 'Oh Well', 'Black Magic Woman', 'Woman Of 1000 Years', 'Homeward Bound', Kirwan's 'Bad Man Blues', and an otherwise unknown song called 'Ride 'Em Cowboys', which might be a misidentification for something else.

Album release: November 1971
UK release of Greatest Hits
This compilation album covers the period from the band's beginning in 1968 to 1971. It was the first time that many of these songs were released on an album. Side one: 'The Green Manalishi (With The Two Prong Crown)', 'Oh Well, Part 1', 'Oh Well, Part 2', 'Shake Your Moneymaker', 'Need Your Love So Bad', 'Rattlesnake Shake'
Side two: 'Dragonfly', 'Black Magic Woman', 'Albatross', 'Man Of The World', 'Stop Messin' Round', 'Love That Burns'

UK Tour
A short UK tour in December 1971 saw Fleetwood Mac playing less-than-salubrious venues, such as the Leys Youth Club in Letchworth and the North London Polytechnic. They didn't arrive for their booking at the Cascadia Ballroom in Ventnor on the Isle of Wight.

1972

Bare Trees
Personnel:
Mick Fleetwood: drums, percussion
Danny Kirwan: guitar, vocals
Christine McVie: keyboards, vocals
John McVie: bass guitar
Bob Welch: guitar, vocals
Recorded 1971–1972 at De Lane Lea Music Centre, Wembley, London (apart from 'Thoughts On A Grey Day' recorded at Mrs Scarrott's home in Hampshire). Produced by Fleetwood Mac.
Album release: March 1972.
Highest chart placings: UK: did not chart US: 70
Side one: 'Child Of Mine', 'The Ghost', 'Homeward Bound', 'Sunny Side Of Heaven'
Side two: 'Bare Trees', 'Sentimental Lady', 'Danny's Chant', 'Spare Me A Little Of Your Love', 'Dust', 'Thoughts On A Grey Day'

'Sentimental Lady' b/w 'Sunny Side Of Heaven'
US Single release May 1972 (did not chart)

'Spare Me A Little' b/w 'Sunny Side Of Heaven'
US Single release August 1972 (did not chart)

Bare Trees is a better-developed, fresher-sounding, tighter and more confident companion album to *Future Games*. The months of cohabitation and/or relentless touring had brought the band together. *Bare Trees* was laid down in the early weeks of 1972 during days off from a four-week British tour. It was just four months since the release of *Future Games*. *Bare Trees* was recorded at De Lane Lea Studios in Wembley – a return to the recording venue of *Kiln House*.

The album opens with Danny Kirwan's 'Child Of Mine': a brisk, confident guitar-led rocker dedicated to his infant son. Kirwan wrote, tellingly, 'I won't leave you, No not like my father did'. 'Danny's Chant' kicks off with overloaded wah-wah guitar and is a heavy rocker reminiscent of the Cream of *Disraeli Gears*. Tim Sommer:

'Danny's Chant', one of the most interesting tracks on *Bare Trees* (even if it's not one of the best), is nothing less than the beta-version of 'Tusk'.

Featuring a tribal Fleetwood beat and some chanted vocals, it's difficult to imagine that Mac weren't aware of it when they recorded the more famous song six years later.

The album's title track is a Grateful Dead/blue-eyed-soul crossover, with a single verse of morose, mournful lyrics: 'Bare trees, gray light/Oh yeah it was a cold night/I was alone in the cold of a winters day/You were alone and so snug in your bed'.
  Bob Welch:

'Bare Trees' does feel lonely, and I don't know how that happened. There was no overall plan to make 'Bare Trees' sound bleak. I think a lot of that mood comes from Danny's angst in his writing. I think maybe Danny's songs always had a kind of loneliness and forlorn-ness to them. He spent a lot of time on the 3rd floor of Benifold, in his room. Sometimes he didn't come down for days. He was a very meticulous guitar player. The notes had to be exactly right. He didn't play any 'b.s.' or twiddly-twiddly-twee licks just to fill time. Danny's style was to make every note count emotionally; no flash fooling around just to impress. This was actually a very mature style to have at a young age. I learned a lot from Danny about 'economy of notes', and really trying to say something in a guitar lead.

Kirwan also wrote the elegant and graceful 'Dust' – a gorgeous piece of music with some deft guitar strokes that uses the opening two stanzas of a 1910 Rupert Brooke poem; macabre words that seemed to reflect Kirwan's darker side.

When the white flame in us is gone
And we that lost the world's delight
Sullen in darkness, left alone
To crumble in our separate night
When your swift hair is quiet in death
And through the lips corruption thrust
Has stilled the labour of my breath –
When we are dust, when we are dust…

Tim Sommer wrote in *The Observer* in 2015

'Dust' lies somewhere between Richard Thompson and Neil Young and has a beach-in-winter, sepia-toned quality to it. It's deeply beautiful and deeply sad, and like many of Kirwan's best songs, it is compact in structure and length but expansive in emotion.

Bob Welch's 'Sentimental Lady' is one of his best-known compositions. It's a tender love song, written for his wife, Nancy, with a fabulous, irrepressibly catchy chorus. Welch: 'It was based on one of those messy girlfriend/boyfriend breakups, that you later wish hadn't happened, and you're sitting alone, wishing it had been different!'.

The song has a mellow, California feel that was new to Fleetwood Mac. The wonderfully commercial male/female counterpoint is also a clear marker to the big Fleetwood Mac hits of the future: it's a mystery why it was ignored by record buyers when it was released as a single in May 1972. Welch re-recorded 'Sentimental Lady' in 1977, with help from Lindsey Buckingham, Christine McVie and Mick Fleetwood. It was, quite rightly, a major solo hit for him.

David Fricke: 'I prefer the original 'Sentimental Lady' on *Bare Trees*. It is warmer and more intimate – in its arrangement and Welch's high fragile vocal – than his later AOR interpretation'.

'The Ghost' is laid-back and acoustic: the chorus is pure Laurel Canyon. The flute parts were played by Christine McVie on a Mellotron.

Christine McVie's two songs are amongst her best so far. 'Homeward Bound', with its pushing-from-behind drum pattern, is a simple wish for a proper night's rest in her own bed. 'I want to sit at home in my rockin' chair/I don't want to travel the world'. She was never too keen on the constant touring. It was, by now, starting to take a toll on her marriage to John: a subject detailed in one of her greatest songs: 'Spare Me A Little Of Your Love'.

This song marks a breakthrough for Christine McVie – the rich lead vocal, the harmonised voices on the chorus (three or perhaps four overdubbed vocals, all McVie), the simple verse/chorus structure, the hand-on-heart lyrics. 'Spare Me A Little Of Your Love' would stay in the band's set until the end of 1975 and would be occasionally performed in 1977 and 1978. It's still a classic.

If *Bare Trees* still sometimes sounds like three (very good) bands on the same album, their style is starting to coalesce, especially on 'Spare Me A Little Of Your Love', 'Sentimental Lady' and Danny Kirwan's masterpiece, 'Sunny Side Of Heaven'. This soaring and beautifully melodic instrumental uses the 'Albatross' guitar sound to devastating effect.

Tim Sommer, once again in the *The Observer* in 2015, said:

'Sunny Side Of Heaven' is a bittersweet, richly melodic instrumental that has a third-Velvet Underground-album-meets-Durutti-Column quality. It's without a doubt one of the ten best Mac songs ever recorded.

A previously unheard outtake from *Bare Trees* – Kirwan's 'Trinity' – was released in 1992 on *25 Years – The Chain*. It's a pulsating blues-rocker which perhaps didn't fit with the sombre tone of the released album. A mono version can be heard on the *1969 to 1974* box set.

Danny Kirwan's nine contributions to the *Future Games* and *Bare Trees* sessions, represented his musical zenith. 'Danny was a producer of music'. Mick Fleetwood said. 'He would have been quite happy creating orchestrations for movies. He never really felt comfortable singing anything.'

Bare Trees closes with two minutes of poetry-reading, which shouldn't work, but somehow does. Bob Welch:

The spoken thing about 'trees so bare, so bare' on *Bare Trees* ('Thoughts On A Grey Day'), was written, I think, by this sweet old lady that lived near Benifold, named Mrs. Scarrott. It was Mick's idea to get her on tape reading her poetry. We just paid her a visit with a cassette tape recorder.

With typical Fleetwood Mac bad luck, the master tapes of the finished album were damaged in transit. Bob Welch wrote:

The *Bare Trees* masters got erased because the airlines had just started putting in anti-hijacking metal detectors, and the very first ones were not 'tape safe' and would erase recorded tapes. They don't do that now! I remember the playback at Warners of the 'erased' tapes; it was embarrassing. All the execs were sitting around in a conference room anticipating the new record, and what they heard sounded like it was underwater ... It was a Maalox moment!

The band needed to recreate the master mix at the Record Plant in Los Angeles. 'The remix may have been slightly different from the one that got erased', said Bob Welch, 'but we never did sit down and compare the 'copy master' with the remix'.

Robert Christgau said, in *Village Voice:*

Their new identity is ominously mellow, but at least this time it's recognizable, and they've upped the speed a little. A lot less muddled than *Future Games* and occasionally as rich as *Kiln House*, but so thoroughly homogenized that it's hard to remember exactly how the cream tasted once it's gone down.

Bud Scoppa said in *Rolling Stone*, on 8 June 1972:

Bare Trees falls somewhere between the last two Fleetwood Macs: that is, it hits harder than *Future Games*, but its concerns are much more introspective than those of *Kiln House*. (Danny) Kirwan has written two melancholic, really elegiac songs based on the bittersweet poem of an elderly woman – 'Thoughts On A Grey Day' – that closes the album. 'Bare Trees' moves along exhilaratingly, even though its lyric is a metaphor of age and approaching death: perhaps it's the acceptance of the cycle that gives the music a hopeful, almost happy feeling. 'Dust' is a great deal more sombre, but it retains Kirwan's deft melodic touch, manifesting itself in both the sighing vocal and in the guitar lines that sweep softly alongside it.

The rest of *Bare Trees* isn't nearly so melancholy, nor is it structured to conform to the theme Kirwan has developed. Christine McVie's two songs, 'Homeward Bound' and 'Spare Me A Little Of Your Love' (which sounds like a hit single to me), make it clear that she's become a fine songwriter and a persuasive vocalist – she's somewhere between Sandy Denny and Dusty Springfield, and there's no doubt that she could make it on her own. Bob Welch's two contributions, however, don't approach the power of 'Future Games'. His 'The Ghost' and 'Sentimental Lady', while not unattractive in themselves, are the weakest tracks on the album. Both are trite.

As before, it's Danny Kirwan who makes the difference. There's nothing on *Bare Trees* to equal 'Station Man' and 'Jewel-Eyed Judy', but, aside from 'Dust', Kirwan's songs here rock much more than his *Future Games* material did. He really lets loose on 'Danny's Chant', which features tough-guy electric guitar sounds purely for their own sake. His 'Child Of Mine' is a lyrically disjointed but musically forthright rock 'n' roll song. And Kirwan's instrumental, 'Sunny Side Of Heaven', shows off his unique electric guitar style to good advantage. Like most outstanding guitarists, Kirwan gets a sound that is more plainly human than mechanical. His guitar tone is piercing but tremulous – powerful but at the same time plaintive, especially in the upper ranges.

The British press had nothing to say.

The British are Coming

Fleetwood Mac spent most of 1972 on tour in the US – a sign that the American market was now their primary focus.

'In England, we may sell five or six thousand (copies of our albums) by the time they are finished, but it's nowhere near what they used to sell', acknowledged Fleetwood to *Melody Maker* in mid-1972.

Following several dates in the UK provinces: their last home turf shows for five years – Bob Welch's reaction to the British winter in Derby, Huddersfield, Folkestone, Sunderland and Leeds has not been recorded – Fleetwood Mac once again travelled across the Atlantic for a major tour of the US and Canada. Billed as 'The British are Coming', a three-band bill crossed the continent from February to April.

Shows would be opened by blues shouter, Long John Baldry, who had had a hit album in the US called *It Ain't Easy*, released in June 1971. He had just recorded its follow-up – *Everything Stops for Tea* – with producers Elton John and Rod Stewart. His band at the time included guitarist Bob Weston, who would join Fleetwood Mac in September 1972.

The closing act was Savoy Brown who, through relentless touring, were the biggest draw on the US circuit at this time. With more line-ups than even Fleetwood Mac, Savoy Brown in 1972 comprised the rhythm section from the Christine Perfect-era Chicken Shack – bassist Andy Silvester and drummer Dave Bidwell – as well as her replacement in that band, Paul Raymond. The line-up was completed by Kim Simmonds – the sole consistent member of Savoy Brown since 1965 and still playing with them today – and singer Dave Walker, previously of The Idle Race. Walker, too, would become a member of Fleetwood Mac by the end of the year.

Fleetwood Mac's hour-long set would follow Long John Baldry's, comprising some or all of 'Tell Me All The Things You Do', 'Get Like You Used To Be' (the Chicken Shack song, with most of that band in the house), 'Sunny Side Of Heaven', 'Future Games', 'Homeward Bound', 'The Ghost', 'Spare Me A Little Of Your Love', 'Child Of Mind', 'Black Magic Woman' and 'Oh Well'. Their set would close with a nod to the bluesy sounds of Savoy Brown and Long John Baldry, with the return of 'Shake Your Moneymaker' from *Peter Green's Fleetwood Mac*. A decent recording of a 55-minute KISW FM radio broadcast from Seattle in March 1972 features most of these songs. There's a version of 'Homeward Bound' included in the *1969 to 1974* box set that eclipses just about any other live recording of the band in this period.

Danny Kirwan leaves Fleetwood Mac

By late August 1972, 22-year old Danny Kirwan had developed an alcohol dependency and was becoming alienated from Welch and the McVies. Something had to give. Mick Fleetwood:

> Danny and Bob got into an argument over Bob's guitar being supposedly out of tune. We were all sitting backstage, getting ready to go on when Danny went off on a rant about Bob never being in tune. Then he got up suddenly, went into the bathroom and smashed his head into the wall, splattering blood everywhere.

Bob Welch recalled the incident:

> We had a university gig somewhere. Danny started to throw this major fit in the dressing room. He had a beautiful guitar. First, he started banging the wall with his fists, then he threw his guitar at the mirror, which shattered, raining glass everywhere. He was pissed out of his brain, which he was for most of the time. We couldn't reason with him.

Kirwan refused to go on stage and watched the concert from the sound desk. The exact date and location of this altercation cannot be pinpointed with accuracy – it might be San Diego, it might not; it might be late August, it might be early September.

'To do a whole set without Danny was tough', Welch recalled later, 'because the arrangements depended on him being there for a guitar part, or vocal part or whatever. I was extremely pissed off. The set seemed to drag on forever. I think we told the audience Danny was 'sick' ... which, I guess he was in a way'.

When Kirwan went backstage and criticised the band afterwards, Mike Fleetwood fired him:

> I couldn't believe he had the nerve to critique our performance. I went to his room and told him we all knew he wasn't happy and that the best thing would be for him to leave the band. He just couldn't relax around people and it made us feel very ill at ease. It became intolerable; everyone was so fucking tense. I finally admitted I couldn't take it either, and I had to be the one to tell him, to put him out of his misery. I knew he wouldn't understand, and he didn't – he asked why. It was horrible. Danny didn't say a word. No one had ever been fired from Fleetwood Mac before. I went

upstairs to John and Christine's room and was crying before I even got to the door.

Welch commented:

Danny Kirwan was a wonderful, brilliant musician, and we had no problem there at all. It was just his personality. (He) wasn't very light-hearted, to say the least. He probably shouldn't have been drinking as much as he did, even at his young age. He was always very intense about his work, as I was, but he didn't seem to ever be able to distance himself from it and laugh about it. Danny was the definition of 'deadly serious'. I thought he was a nice kid, but a little bit paranoid, a little bit disturbed. He would always take things I said wrongly. He would take offence at things for no reason ... I thought it was just me, but as I got to know the rest of the band, they'd say, 'Oh yes, Danny, a little ... strange'. He was 'ill' I think, even then. In the end, Danny was making all of us feel very uncomfortable. But he was a talented, gifted musician, almost equal to Peter Green in his beautiful guitar-playing and faultless string bends.

Much later, Christine McVie had this to say of the guitarist: 'He was really, really neurotic and difficult to work with – he was one of those people that would never look you in the eye'.

John McVie: 'Danny Kirwan. He was quite a player. Lovely vibrato. Danny was very young when he joined us. A very nice guy, nervous and shy, but what a player! He had a lot of insecurity that emerged over time. More so with success and pressure.'

Bob Welch agreed: 'He was always very isolated, very sensitive, and frankly he was very difficult to get to know'.

Kirwan later said, in a rare interview with Martin Celmins:

I always liked Mick Fleetwood – he was like family, but nowadays it's a bit distant, you know, people living in different cities. But I still think of them as friends. John McVie is the cleverest person and I could see that at the time. A nice bloke and highly intelligent, he was like my best friend in the band for a time. The thing with rock bands is that they get very interested in themselves and their own relationships with each other – a cliquey kind of thing. Spencer and Green, for instance, knew each other well and were ... mischievous. It was a very mischievous band. So I wasn't actually a part of them, really. I only got mixed up with them.

Officially the band's announcement read:

> Danny's music was getting further away from what Mac wanted to play.
> After spending a lot of time playing exhaustive tours of America, it was felt
> that new blood and fresh ideas were needed in the band. Danny was happy
> to leave because he wanted to do a solo album for some time and he is
> now working on this project.

Kirwan went on to record three solo albums between 1975 and 1979.
During the 1980s and 1990s, he was homeless in London. In 1993, Kirwan
spoke to the *Evening Standard* and said, 'I've been through a bit of a
rough patch, but I'm not too bad. I get by and I suppose I am homeless,
but then I've never really had a home since our early days on tour'. He
added, with a touch of pathos, 'If Mick would like to see me, that would
be nice'. Fleetwood subsequently contacted the Missing Persons Bureau
in London, from Los Angeles, and Kirwan was traced to a hostel where he
had lived for the past four years.

In a 1994 interview, Peter Green said of Kirwan: 'I think Mick and I
are responsible for where he is now. I wish I could help him, but I don't
know how'.

In poor mental and physical health for many years, Danny Kirwan died
in London, on 8 June 2018, aged 68. A 'best of' album of Kirwan's work
with Fleetwood Mac would be very strong: 'Jigsaw Puzzle Blues' (B-side
of 'Albatross'); 'Something Inside Of Me' from *English Rose*; 'Coming Your
Way' from *Then Play On*; 'Jewel-Eyed Judy' and 'Tell Me All The Things
You Do' from *Kiln House*; 'Dragonfly' (single)'; Sands Of Time', 'Woman
Of 1,000 Years' and 'Sometimes' from *Future Games*; 'Child Of Mine',
'Dust' and 'Sunny Side Of Heaven' from *Bare Trees*; 'Trinity' from the
Bare Trees sessions.

Kirwan's departure from Fleetwood Mac was the third major change
since May 1970. But if the previous two and a half years had been difficult
for Fleetwood Mac, the next two and a half years would be chaotic.

Dave Walker and Bob Weston

Mick Fleetwood's instinct had brought Bob Welch to Fleetwood Mac.
The recruitment of the versatile, charismatic Bob Weston was similarly
inspired.

'We needed a replacement for Danny', Fleetwood wrote in his memoirs.
'And we found one in Bob Weston.'

'It was great; being the new boy', Weston said later. 'It was all a new experience. I deferred to their talents; I was the baby writer, just starting out.'

The band's other new boy was singer Dave Walker.

'Getting Dave Walker was our manager Clifford Davis' idea', claimed Mick Fleetwood in *Q*. 'We've got to get a lead singer out front who can start boogieing!' Dave did a good job and sounded great alongside Weston's slide guitar.'

Bob Welch: 'There was a lot of pressure from Davis to be a 'star-quality', headlining act. He saw bands like Deep Purple ... macho, heavy bands with a lead singer strutting around the stage – and he thought we should have a front man'.

Both Weston and Walker had been part of the three-band The British Are Coming tour across the US earlier in the year: Weston with Long John Baldry, and Walker with Savoy Brown. Walker would spend just ten months in Fleetwood Mac; Weston another four.

Bob Weston said later:

Leaving Long John Baldry for Fleetwood Mac was a natural progression. It was an amicable parting of the ways. Being surrounded by so much creative writing talent (in Fleetwood Mac) – Bob Welch, Christine McVie, and a very serious rhythm section – was perfection for a guitarist like myself. It seemed I'd been building up for years to hit this zenith. Bullseye! In addition, it was a wonderful opportunity to tour America on a very professional level. I learned a lot. Dave and I joined on the same day; we were the new boys. It looked very promising from the start. Dave's forte was as a frontman, in live performance. We all felt he was the right man for the job.

Despite the brevity of Weston's tenure with Fleetwood Mac, his contribution was immense. His lyrical, fluid guitar-playing was a perfect fit for the band's more relaxed, West Coast sound, especially on *Mystery to Me*.

Exact dates for Walker's and Weston's debuts are uncertain. Fleetwood Mac were performing almost every night from 14 August to 9 September, then from 14 to 16 September, 23, 29 and 30 September and 1 October, the end of their current tour. It seems unlikely that they would have flown two new members to the US, mid-tour.

Fleetwood Mac spent October off the road: the likeliest period for bedding in Dave Walker and Bob Weston. 'Initial rehearsals were full of energy'. Weston recalled. 'This was further endorsed with the initial tour, structured to break us in as a team. Dave would sing the heavier songs like 'Going Down' and 'Roadrunner', which would feature his harmonica-playing. Probably a couple more standard blues, but the titles evade me.'

Walker recalls:

> I sang 'Rattlesnake Shake' and 'Oh Well'. In some respects, I thought that perhaps I would be able to perform songs of that type with the band, but with Bob Welch and Christine doing the bulk of the writing and with their unique styles, that was not to be. I thought that joining Fleetwood Mac after fronting Savoy Brown – which was a much more successful band in the US at the time – I would be allowed to impress my style and personality on the band to greater effect. When I did join the band, my role was never that clearly defined. With Savoy Brown, basically I did all the singing. With Fleetwood Mac, suddenly I was singing with two other people. Maybe there were just too many singers.

American Tour

Fleetwood Mac flew back to the US for another seven weeks of live dates in November and December 1972, again supporting Deep Purple.

'To my knowledge, there are no sanctioned live recordings of (this line-up of) the band', Dave Walker suggests.

'During our last house move a few months ago', John McVie said recently, 'I found a box full of old soundboard cassettes. I think there's one with Dave Walker on it. So that shows you how old they are. I bought an 'analog-to-digital' transfer unit, but haven't got 'round to putting them on CD. The band has no plans to release anything like this. So maybe I'll start a company, sell them on eBay, piss the band off and make a fortune'.

The tour visited New York, Philadelphia, Connecticut, Virginia, Illinois, Missouri, Oklahoma, California, Texas, Iowa, Indiana, Minnesota, Ohio, Michigan, Alabama, Arkansas and Florida: 29 shows in 45 days. It ended at the Academy of Music in New York City on 23 December 1972, on an eclectic bill with Elephant's Memory, best known for backing John Lennon and Yoko Ono; progressive folk-rockers, McKendree Spring, and British jazz and blues saxophonist, Dick Heckstall-Smith.

Bob Weston: 'Then the *Penguin* sessions began, and so did the doubts.'

1973

Penguin
Personnel:
Mick Fleetwood: drums, percussion
Christine McVie: keyboards, vocals
John McVie: bass guitar
Dave Walker: vocals, harmonica
Bob Welch: guitar, vocals, bass guitar
Bob Weston: lead guitar, slide guitar, banjo, harmonica, harmony vocals
Peter Green: additional lead guitar on 'Night Watch'
Steve Nye: organ on 'Night Watch'
Ralph Richardson, Russell Valdez and Fred Totesant: steel drums on 'Did You Ever Love Me'
Recorded January-February 1973 with the Rolling Stones' Mobile Studio at Benifold, Hampshire.
Produced by Fleetwood Mac and Martin Birch.
Album release: March 1973.
Highest chart placings: UK: did not chart, US: 49
Side one: 'Remember Me', 'Bright Fire', 'Dissatisfied', '(I'm A) Road Runner'
Side two: 'The Derelict', 'Revelation', 'Did You Ever Love Me', 'Night Watch', 'Caught In The Rain'

'Remember Me' b/w 'Dissatisfied'
US Single release May 1973 (did not chart)

'Albatross' b/w 'Need Your Love So Bad'
UK Re-release single release: May 1973
This re-release reached number two in the UK charts w/c 23 June 1973 during a fifteen-week chart run.

'Did You Ever Love Me' b/w 'The Derelict'
UK single release July 1973 (did not chart)

'Did You Ever Love Me' b/w 'Revelation'
US Single release September 1973 (did not chart)

'*Penguin* was recorded at Fleetwood Mac's house south of London', recalls Dave Walker. 'I spent much of my time in the local bar.'

'It was a cold winter', Bob Welch said, 'and we used the Rolling Stones' Mobile Unit to record (at Benifold)'.

'Being at Benifold was ideal', recalled Bob Weston. 'A great rehearsal situation, plenty of space, lots of lovely food, and a great little pub down the road.'

Dave Walker said:

I did not move in to Benifold, as I had a place in London. But we did stay there at the house most of the time when we were rehearsing and recording. I have to say that it was a frustrating time for me, as I was involved with people that I liked, but was unable to contribute for one reason or another. The two songs that I did on the album were, in my opinion, somewhat of an afterthought, and with no disrespect to the other band members, I never really felt very comfortable. Becoming the frontman for Fleetwood Mac was kind of redundant, as Christine and Bob Welch were already performing that function, and so I was never used as that.

Walker sang lead on two songs on *Penguin*. According to Samuel Graham, they were 'as egregious as a wart on Cybill Shepherd' with their version of Junior Walker's '(I'm a) Road Runner', adding it was 'one of the worst tracks Fleetwood Mac has ever done'.

Walker said later:

'Road Runner' was just a suggestion from the band. I thought 'Road Runner' was a decent choice of song for me to sing, but again, it was done very quickly, and the vocals did leave a lot to be desired. There were no covers other than 'Road Runner' ever performed by me with the band, and I think we only played that song a few times live.

'Those who complain about the remake of '(I'm A) Road Runner'', noted Robert Christgau in 1973, 'with Mick Fleetwood smashing past the cymbals while Dave Walker shouts, probably think these studio craftspeople were slumming when they jammed with Otis Spann. I love it'.

In truth, '(I'm A) Road Runner' is a decent cover: Walker can belt out a blues, his harmonica wails effectively, Weston and Welch's guitars weave around each other to great effect, and, of course, the McVie/McVie/Fleetwood rhythm section is peerless. It's simply unnecessary.

Walker's original song, 'The Derelict', takes Fleetwood Mac towards folk-rock: think Gallagher and Lyle, or the rootsier songs of The Band.

''The Derelict' was written from a life experience and did have personal connotations for me at the time', he wrote later. 'The song on the album was never finished, as there was no bass track and there was no real production.'

On its own terms, 'The Derelict' is a terrific little song. But, as with '(I'm A) Road Runner', it's utterly out of place on a 1973 Fleetwood Mac album. Two good-to-great songs – wrong place, wrong time.

'I had very little contribution on the finished product', Walker says. 'I must admit that I was, at best, ambivalent about it. I do not want you to think that there is any bitterness present, but my thoughts on the album are just a personal matter of fact.'

Christine McVie contributes two fine songs that sit more easily in the Fleetwood Mac milieu. The breezy 'Remember Me' opens the album. Bob Weston's lovely slide guitar embellishes a strong McVie lead vocal. 'Dissatisfied' is a highlight of the album: a biting song with a punchy rhythm that would later underpin 'Don't Stop'. She harmonises with herself in the choruses: if Buckingham and Nicks were in place then, this song would sit happily on *Fleetwood Mac* or *Rumours*. Weston's guitar solo is excellent, full of country bends and twangs.

Bob Welch's three songs are typically wordy, worldly, thoughtful and complex. 'Bright Fire' has a soft, jazzy feel. John McVie's bass provides almost a second melody, and again, Bob Weston embellishes the melody with guitar flourishes.

Bob Welch: 'Bright Fire' was indirectly about the cruelties, on both sides, in the Vietnam war, and how could all that suffering be 'redeemed' – what was it for? It was very abstract, though. 'The rose that will be growing' is sort of a metaphor, like the Christian one, for death and resurrection'.

Don't let waters of caution remove you
Don't let the fire of saints compel you
Don't let the lack of their spirit blind your life
'Cause soon it's all over, you're gonna come through alive

'Revelation' has a depth of production that looks forward to *Rumours*: furiously strummed acoustic guitar, bopping congas, a spiralling guitar solo. Bob Welch plays bass. It could be a lost Santana outtake.

'I feel I need to clear my friend Mr. McVie's name', says Dave Walker, 'as I think his drinking habits have been grossly exaggerated. But it may well be that Bob Welch did play the bass track on 'Revelation', but I cannot be sure as I was in the bar. Whether John was with me or not has long since been erased from my memory bank'.

The catchy, ambitious pop-rock, 'Night Watch', is not so far from 'Sentimental Lady', despite its sometimes knotty lyrics ('Cause I have lived alone in castles that were lonely/And I have cursed the dawn and wondered why I do/Well I have wondered why I live/Now I know you must forgive/Let me stand inside your magic shadow'). The chorus is pure Crosby, Stills & Nash. Fleetwood Mac's founding guitarist Peter Green makes a guest appearance, playing unmistakable lead breaks in the central section and at the end.

'Peter plays some eerie stuff way in the background on 'Night Watch', Bob Welch recalled. 'He was there at the studio with the rest of us when he did it ... he actually played the part standing in the studio's echo chamber.'

Dave Walker: 'He nailed the track on the second take. Truly magical.'
Bob Weston:

I remember it clearly; it was at Air Studios in Oxford Street in London. Peter would occasionally pop in to the studio to see how we were doing; inevitably a jam session would ensue.

'Did You Ever Love Me' is a unique Christine McVie/Bob Welch co-write. It's sung by McVie with Bob Weston, and their voices work brilliantly together: here's another of the elements of the radio-friendly Fleetwood Mac sound in utero. The steel drums are perhaps an overdub too far.
Bob Welch:

Weston sang with Christine on 'Did You Ever ... ' either, 1: because he had been a naughty boy and we wanted to torture him ... 2: he was in one of his 'giddy' moods, and needed something to do ... 3: Dave Walker and I were having a drunken brawl, and couldn't be disturbed, or 4: we had forgotten to formally 'audition' Bob, and this was his big chance at the 'Engelbert Humperdinck' thing we all knew he was capable of!

The album closes with Bob Weston's gentle acoustic instrumental, 'Caught In The Rain'.

So, *Penguin*: A solid album that has aged well. It's chock full of great songs, but there are those two cuckoos in the nest. It's perhaps not quite as good as *Future Games* or *Bare Trees* – Danny Kirwan casts a long shadow – but the addition of Bob Weston was an astute move. His tasteful and inventive guitar skills perfectly complemented the songs of Christine McVie and Bob Welch.

Penguin was the highest-charting Fleetwood Mac album in the US at the time, edging its way into the Top 50 at 49.

Mystery to Me

Personnel:
Mick Fleetwood: drums, percussion
Christine McVie: keyboards, vocals
John McVie: bass guitar
Bob Welch: guitar, vocals, bass guitar
Bob Weston: lead guitar, slide guitar, backing vocals
Recorded Spring-Summer 1973 on the Rolling Stones' Mobile Studio at Benifold, Hampshire; mixed at Advision Studios, London.
Produced by Fleetwood Mac and Martin Birch.
Album release: 15 October 1973.
Highest chart placings: UK: did not chart , US: 67
Side one: 'Emerald Eyes', 'Believe Me', 'Just Crazy Love', 'Hypnotised', 'Forever', 'Keep On Going'
Side two: 'The City', 'Miles Away', 'Somebody', 'The Way I Feel', 'For Your Love', 'Why?'

'For Your Love' b/w 'Hypnotised'

US single release December 1973 (did not chart)
UK single release March 1974 (did not chart)

Back in the UK after a three-month US tour, Fleetwood Mac recorded their eighth album in spring and summer 1973, again utilising the Rolling Stones' Mobile studio at Benifold. *Mystery to Me* is ambitious, varied, and very good indeed. The songs are strong and confident, and this sounds like a band who are working well together.

Bob Welch: 'The *Mystery to Me* album stands out as the most 'solid' album, all the way through, that I did with Fleetwood Mac. *Mystery* ... is the one I'd take with me to a desert island'.

It is Welch's 'Hypnotised' that is perhaps the best song here. According to Richie Unterberger, it has 'a gently percolating and aptly hypnotic rhythm gliding into an unforgettable chorus that – like the big hits Fleetwood Mac would land a few years later – craftily combined layers of male and female vocals'.

'Hypnotised' is a key link in Fleetwood Mac's progression from 1960s blues to a commercial mid-1970s AM-friendly behemoth. But it was initially a much harder-rocking song planned as a showcase for Dave Walker.

'There were two tracks that I originally recorded vocals on', Dave Walker wrote later. 'One was Christine's song, and I think one was Bob Welch's. I would doubt that my tracks were kept, although if my memory serves me well, my performances were good.'

But Walker's rhythm and blues style did not fit the newer, smoother sound of Fleetwood Mac. He was asked to leave in mid-1973 during sessions for *Mystery to Me*.

'Dave was great in Savoy Brown', Christine McVie said in 1978. 'But you try and get a guy like Dave Walker singing anything other than Howlin' Wolf or Freddie King or rock and roll boogie, and he just didn't cut it. He wasn't terribly versatile, that's all, and he wasn't right for us.'

'Dave would go down the pub and get drunk while we (tried) desperately to figure out what we could give him to do', Bob Welch commented. 'The light finally dawned on us that we were throwing away what Fleetwood Mac had been, that we weren't Savoy Brown. It was an experiment that failed.'

'In fairness to Fleetwood Mac', Walker says, 'I was pretty burned out and was having problems of my own at the time, which restricted my effectiveness in all areas of my life, both professional and personal. And so, as history has shown, my involvement with Fleetwood Mac was never what it could have been'.

'Dave was only interested in writing songs that sounded like Savoy Brown', Mick Fleetwood says.

Walker said later: 'I didn't feel like a full member of Fleetwood Mac, although that may have been just my own paranoia. As Bob Weston said, 'I did feel like a fish out of water, more like a fish in beer'.'

'Dave's raw British R&B style didn't blend with the way the band was tending in its direction', said Bob Weston. 'We were seeking a new sound.'

A version of a mid-period classic such as 'Hypnotised', being sung by Dave Walker, is one we can only imagine. Bob Welch:

I don't know if there is a (surviving) take of Dave Walker doing 'Hypnotised'. I would assume that an engineer never erases any final vocals, but if there is one, I've never heard it, or heard about it. When we realised that Dave was not fitting in musically with what we were trying to do, I hurriedly rewrote the lyrics in Christine McVie's upstairs living room at Benifold. The 'playing field' mentioned in one of the verses made a reference to the large grass tennis court, which was part of the property ... and kind of spooky at night. I was interested in the paranormal – UFOs, the Carlos Castaneda books about the Yaqui Indian 'sorcerer', Don Juan – so I incorporated a lot of these themes and references into the song. The 'place down in Mexico' refers to Castaneda's Yaqui sorcerer, Don Juan, who is presumably doing 'astral' travel. The 'strange, strange pond' with 'sides like glass' refers to a strange anomalous depression in the woods near Winston-Salem, North Carolina, which a friend told me about, which, at the time, freaked him out. 'Hypnotised' is not a drum loop. Mick copied my Maestro Rhythm machine part almost exactly. His sense of tempo, in this day before drum machines, was almost perfect. Talk about 'carpal tunnel', I don't know how he did it! Mick was one of the few drummers who could have pulled off being a 'human drum loop'. The cymbals are all what Mick played on the spot, not recorded later. (It's a) favourite song from the old days. It had the 'magic'.

We should also point out Bob Weston's fluid, jazz-influenced guitar solo and Christine McVie's understated electric piano on this important song. 'Hypnotised' would stay in the band's set for several years, even after Welch's departure. Two live versions have been released in recent years: at the Record Plant, Sausalito, in mid-December 1974 for radio broadcast, released in 2020 on the *1969 to 1974* box set; and at Jorgensen Auditorium, University of Connecticut in Storrs, on 25 October 1975, with Lindsey Buckingham on guitar and vocals, released in 2018 on the deluxe edition of *Fleetwood Mac*. David Fricke:

> The best song Welch ever gave the Mac, 'Hypnotised', was urgent noir propelled by a shuffling mix of guitars, with Welch singing in a sleepwalking cadence like a Raymond Chandler detective musing to himself in a late-night rain.

'('Hypnotised' is) classic Bob Welch from a relatively unknown era of Fleetwood Mac that goes overlooked', said Mick Fleetwood. 'This is also the beginning of the vocal harmonies, which later became our trademark.'
 Surely hit single material, Warner Brothers, in their wisdom, released 'Hypnotised' as a B-side.

Mystery to Me includes another five expressive, imaginative songs written by Bob Welch: 'Emerald Eyes', 'The City', 'Miles Away', 'Somebody' and 'Keep On Going'. 'Emerald Eyes', the album's opener, has a clean radio-friendly production. The backing vocals in the chorus leaven Welch's typically breathy vocal. Bob Weston plays some superb guitar breaks.

Bob Welch: 'A lot of times in my songs, I used 'she' to symbolize 'longing', spiritual or otherwise ... 'Emerald Eyes' is like the science fiction 'super-female' with light beams coming out of her eyes, who has all-knowledge, all-sensuality, all-beauty wrapped up in 'her' one super-person'.

'Somebody' has some jazzy chords, a soulful groove and a phased lead vocal. It's little more than a riff, as is the raucous, bluesy 'The City', which has flowing slide guitar and pumping bass. Like 'The City', 'Miles Away' is driven by John McVie's astonishing bass-playing. It features some of Welch's more obscure lyrics: 'Don Juan goes up in a cloud of smoke/ And all those Hare Krishnas turned out to be a joke/And it's restless, restless, restless all the time/Slidin' up and down the surface of this life'. The chorus, though, is as catchy as any other song in the Fleetwood Mac catalogue.

Welch's 'Keep On Going' is sung by Christine McVie. It includes an awesome acoustic guitar solo by Bob Weston and bass by Bob Welch. It's embellished by swooping strings.

Bob Welch:

Christine sung 'Keep On Going' because she liked it and sounded better on it than me. I've always written some things that I personally couldn't sing particularly well. The strings are a real orchestra, arranged I think, by Paul Buckmaster, who did a lot of the early Elton John albums. I probably 'hummed' some lines to either Buckmaster or his copyist, just to give him an idea of the kind of thing we wanted on the song.

Christine McVie matched Welch with 'Believe Me', 'Just Crazy Love', 'The Way I Feel', and the classic 'Why?'. The first two songs named are comments on her not-so-secret extramarital relationship with engineer, Martin Birch.

Bob Welch: '*Mystery to Me* was made with the 'astral' help of some extreme sexual 'zingers' going on between Chris (McVie) and engineer, Martin Birch. These kinds of 'vibes', although upsetting in some ways, can be great for musical creativity'.

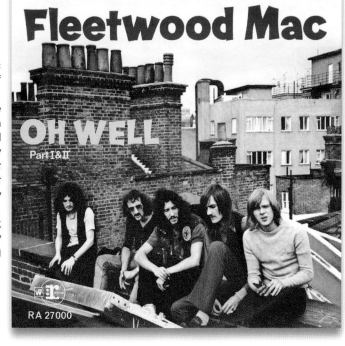

Right: The classic late 60s line-up of Fleetwood Mac, shown here on the 1969 single 'Oh Well'. They would stay together for only twenty months but release three brilliant singles. L to R: Jeremy Spencer, John McVie, Peter Green, Mick Fleetwood, Danny Kirwan. (*Warners*)

Left: Five or so years later, a very different Fleetwood Mac prepare to conquer the world. L to R: Mick Fleetwood, Christine McVie, John McVie, Lindsay Buckingham, Stevie Nicks. (*Warners*)

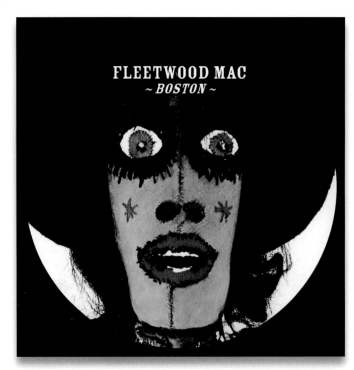

Left: Recorded in February 1970, the *Boston* album was shelved for years. These are brilliantly-mixed live recordings that practically fizz with energy. *(Warners)*

Right: *Kiln House* (1970) was the last Fleetwood Mac album to make the UK charts for five years. It's an album of two contrasting halves: almost two bands with the same players. *(Warners)*

Right: This impressive line up for a festival in April 1970 promised an entertaining day in Reading out for a pound. The concert was cancelled. (*Author's Collection*)

The ***SPRING THING*** is on **APRIL 25th** at Reading Football Stadium, Elm Park, Norfolk Rd., Reading
MID-DAY—7 p.m.
with
fleetwood mac
CHICKEN SHACK   **JON HISEMANS**   **MIKE COOPER**
VIV STANSHALLS BIG GRUNT   **COLOSSEUM**   **CHRISTINE PERFECT**
LIVERPOOL SCENE   COMPERE MIKE RAVEN
TICKETS £1 AVAILABLE
FROM ALL BRANCHES OF HARLEQUIN RECORD SHOPS, XPLOR, READING AND OXFORD, OR READING FOOTBALL CLUB.

To Reading Football Club, Elm Park, Norfolk Road, Reading.
Please send me .... tickets for the Spring Thing.
I enclose £ .... (cheques, P.O.'s payable to Reading Football Club Ltd.) and stamped, addressed envelope.
Name ....
Address ....

Right: A press ad for one of three dates in a short tour of Scotland in April 1970. (*Author's Collection*)

!!! ANDY LOTHIAN Presents
FLEETWOOD MAC
and THE JOHN DUMMER BAND !! !! !!
CAIRD HALL
TUESDAY 21 APRIL 8 P.M.
TICKETS 10/- 15/- 20/- and 25/-
FROM ANDY LOTHIAN ORG. LTD.
31 EXCHANGE STREET, DUNDEE
Please note Peter Green is leaving Fleetwood Mac — but not until AFTER the Dundee concert. Make sure you don't miss one of the last original appearances of this legendary group.

FLEETWOOD MAC
Dragonfly The Purple Dancer
R7-541568

©1971 Reprise Records, a division of Warner Bros. Records Inc.

Left: 'Dragonfly' was a standalone single from March 1971. It is embellished by Danny Kirwan's delicate, exquisite guitar parts. (*Warners*)

Future Games.

Left: *Future Games* introduced Bob Welch to Fleetwood Mac. It's a brilliant album, but no one was listening. (*Warners*)

Right: The magnificent *Bare Trees*: a better-developed, fresher-sounding, tighter and more confident companion album to *Future Games*. (*Warners*)

Right: With Kirwan gone, the band recruited Bob Weston and Dave Walker for *Penguin* (1973). It's a solid album that has aged well, chock full of great songs. (*Warners*)

Left: '*Mystery to Me* was probably the best Fleetwood Mac album since Peter Green had left the band three years earlier', Mick Fleetwood wrote. He's not wrong. With 'Why?', Christine McVie finally finds her perfect style. (*Warners*)

Left: Peter Green. He replaced Eric Clapton in John Mayall's Bluesbreakers in 1966. Green's playing was less aggressive than Clapton's but otherwise equal in every respect. And, at times, better.

Right: Jeremy Spencer. In 2015, Tim Sommer of *The Observer* memorably described Spencer as 'an elfin devotee of amphetamine rockabilly, whose persona seems to presage Dr. Feelgood'.

Left: The 1968-1970 line-up perform the timeless 'Albatross'.

Right: Danny Kirwan, a mesmerising talent but a fragile personality.

Left: Christine McVie, the heart and soul of Fleetwood Mac.

Right: Bob Welch, an intelligent man and a fine musician. His contribution to Fleetwood Mac's five albums over almost four years between April 1971 and December 1974 should not be underestimated.

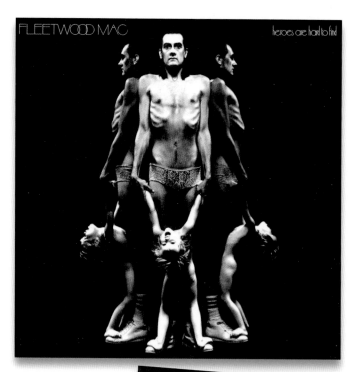

Left: Recorded in Los Angeles, *Heroes Are Hard* To Find points directly to the massive success that the band would soon enjoy. (Warners)

Right: The four-piece Fleetwood Mac of 1973-1974. Bob Welch, John McVie (front), Mick Fleetwood (rear), Christine McVie. (*Warners*)

Right: *1969-1974* is an eight CD box set released in 2020. It includes all of the band's albums and singles during this fruitful period. (*Warners*)

FLEETWOOD MAC

1969 *to* 1974

THEN PLAY ON • KILN HOUSE • FUTURE GAMES • BARE TREES
PENGUIN • MYSTERY TO ME • HEROES ARE HARD TO FIND
LIVE FROM THE RECORD PLANT, DECEMBER 15, 1974

Left: *Fleetwood Mac.* Christine McVie: 'I couldn't believe how great this three-voice harmony was. My skin turned to goose flesh, and I wondered how long this feeling was going to last'. (*Warners*)

Left: Stevie Nicks. The success of 'Rhiannon' and the focus on Stevie Nicks extended the band's reach as teenage girls started to buy Fleetwood Mac records for the first time.

Right: Mick Fleetwood, the band's de facto leader since 1970. His instincts sometimes bordered on genius but at other times resulted in utter chaos.

Left: Stevie Nicks and Lindsay Buckingham. Before joining Fleetwood Mac, Nicks worked as a waitress and cleaner while Buckingham sold ads over the phone.

Right: John McVie. Just along for the ride, really.

Left: Stevie Nicks and Lindsay Buckingham. '*Rumours* sold a storyline', writes Rob Trucks. 'No review, interview or feature about the band was written without assessing the recent break-up of Christine McVie from John McVie, of Stevie Nicks from Lindsey Buckingham. And how the songs of *Rumours* sprang from these separations.'

Right: Christine McVie, writer of mature, mid-paced love songs:' Say You Love Me', 'Over My Head', Warm Ways', 'Sugar Daddy', 'Songbird', 'Oh Daddy', 'Over & Over', 'Think About Me', 'Brown Eyes', 'Never Make Me Cry' and 'Never Forget'.

WB 16 872 Ⓝ

FLEETWOOD MAC
Aus der LP "Rumours" Warner Bros. 56 344
Go Your Own Way
Silver Springs

Von der WEA Musik GmbH ⓦ Eine Warner Communications Gesellschaft · Made in Germany   JAN. '77

Left: 'Go Your Own Way was the first single from *Rumours*, released in December 1976. Says Lindsay Buckingham: 'It really broke the ice and set the tone for the album in general. It got everyone off on the right foot and let everyone feel that we had a strong place to go.' (*Warners*)

Right: *Rumours*. 40 million sales and counting. (*Warners*)

FLEETWOOD MAC
RUMOURS

Right: Stevie Nicks and Mick Fleetwood. 'Mick is definitely one of my great, great loves', Nicks said. 'But that really wasn't good for anybody.' (*Warners*)

Left: John McVie, Lindsay Buckingham, Stevie Nicks, Mick Fleetwood and Christine McVie on the rear cover of *Rumours*. (*Warners*)

Left: Stevie Nicks interviewed for the Australian ABC TV show *Countdown* in 1977. 'Gold Dust Woman', 'Rhiannon' and 'Sara' kick-started a long and successful solo career. (*ABC*)

Right: Mick Fleetwood and Lindsay Buckingham interviewed by *Countdown* during sessions for *Tusk*.

Left: Christine McVie and Stevie Nicks in June 1979, recording the marching band of the University of Southern California for *Tusk's* title track.

Right: The double album *Tusk* is full of great songs but is let down by deliberately jarring sequencing. (*Warners*)

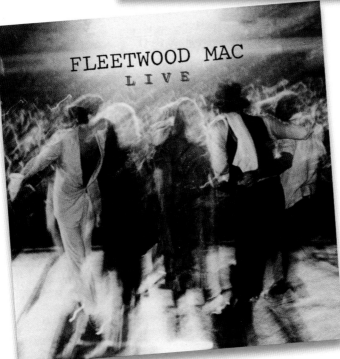

Left: The inevitable live album, recorded in 1975, 1977, 1979 and 1980. 'The Farmer's Daughter' is a studio outtake from April 1979. (*Warners*)

Left: The first *Greatest Hits* album covers the 1967-1971 period of Fleetwood Mac. A second from 1988 had a totally different tracklist. (*Warners*)

Right: The release of *Live At The BBC* by The Beatles in 1994 alerted fans to a so-far untapped wealth of unusual and often unheard live-in-the-studio performances recorded for BBC radio. Fleetwood Mac's BBC album has many worthwhile rare performances. (*BBC*)

Left: Fleetwood Mac show no signs of stopping just yet, despite Lindsey Buckingham being summarily fired in 2018. *50 Years – Don't Stop* is Fleetwood Mac's first career-spanning collection, fifty songs recorded between 1967 and 2013. (Warners)

Oh, when will we be together
In this crazy world we're in?
Is it really such a sin to love you?
Well I've tried my best, but it may not be enough.

'Believe Me' drives hard – Christine's piano-playing is terrific here – and Bob Weston adds a wonderful slide guitar solo. 'Just Crazy Love' is proto-*Rumours*, but is let down by an undeveloped chorus. Much better is 'The Way I Feel', a delightful song which keeps it simple with piano, acoustic guitar, choral backing vocals and a brilliant lead vocal. Hints of 'Over My Heart' and 'Songbird' can be heard.

'Why?' is an out-and-out classic: one of those Fleetwood Mac songs that you can listen to over and over. Bob Weston's splendid slide guitar opens a yearning song, which should be right at the top of everyone's Fleetwood Mac playlist.

There's no use in crying, it's all over
But I know there'll always be another day
Well my heart will rise up with the morning sun
And the hurt I feel will simply melt away

It's a song for John. Finally, Christine McVie has found her perfect style.

Bob Weston: 'From the *Mystery to Me* album: I like 'Why?'. I asked one or two of the band to give me an hour or so while I finished the guitar parts, as Christine was getting a trifle concerned about the way her song was going. Upon their return, everyone had a smile on the dial. Sadly, I missed out on the arrangement credits, as they brought in a string arranger who had my parts played, practically note for note, on strings, and he took the credit. Bummer, eh?'.

David Fricke: 'There was one other diamond on *Mystery*, at the very end: Christine's aching ballad, 'Why?', with its oddly affecting blend of bottleneck guitar and cocktail-piano reverie. It was a hint of the pop-with-twists that would soon transform Fleetwood Mac, and its fortunes with the arrival of Stevie Nicks and Lindsey Buckingham'.

'Why?' would be a highlight of the band's 1975 tour, with Buckingham and Nicks' backing vocals propelling the song into the higher echelons of this band's best-ever tracks.

The album is rounded out by 'Forever', a fun lilting Weston/Welch/Fleetwood/John McVie co-composition with a reggae rhythm, and a

creditable, if expendable, cover of Graham Gouldman's 'For Your Love'.
Bob Welch:

Forever' is one of those little mood pieces that wasn't written at all
beforehand and was the result of a jam between me and John. John McVie
was one of the most inventive bass players I ever worked with. 'Forever'
was really about one little magic moment when the winter English sun
finally came out, and we all rushed outside, and for twenty minutes felt
like we were floating on an island in the Caribbean, watching the all too
infrequent English sunbeams ... which are a lot politer and reserved than
American ones!

John McVie: 'Forever' came about at Benifold. I was down in the Big
Room playing along to a drum machine, and I think it was Chris who
heard the riff I was playing. She liked it and took it from there. I think Bob
Weston had a part in that as well'.
'John really made his bass lines count', Bob Welch said. 'They're almost
like little songs within the song and were always very memorable in
themselves. The atmosphere during the entire recording of *Mystery to Me*,
including 'Forever', was warm, cozy and spacey, very nice.'
Bob Welch:

'For Your Love' was always my favourite Yardbirds song. The Fleetwood Mac
version was another one of those times when I feel the record company let
a potential hit single 'get away'.

There was also a thirteenth song that was recorded for, but left off,
Mystery to Me. It's a Bob Welch song called 'Good Things (Come To Those
Who Wait)'.
'Warners heard the album', Bob Welch remembered. 'They said 'Great...
but there's no single'. So we recorded 'For Your Love' specifically to be
a single. Of course, 'Hypnotised' wound up getting the most radio play.
Warners didn't think 'Hypnotised' was 'commercial' enough to be a
single.'
The change from 'Good Things' to 'For Your Love' came so late that the
album sleeve had already been printed.
'There are two different versions of the album cover', Bob Welch wrote.
'The very first cover that was printed listed a song of mine, 'Good Things',
on it. Then we got to L.A. and decided to replace 'Good Things' with 'For

Your Love'. But it was too late to recall some of the first covers that had already been printed. If you had a vinyl copy of *Mystery to Me* with the song 'Good Things' listed on it, you have one of only a very few like that.'

Welch later reworked 'Good Things' as 'Don't Wait Too Long', on his album *Three Hearts*: 'Sometimes song fragments would hang around for quite a few years, without getting used, and then I would find a way to bring them together for a new song'.

The Fleetwood Mac version – with its odd chord changes, ethereal backing vocals, driving drum pattern and hints of 'Albatross' guitar – would be released in 2020 as part of the *1969 to 1974* box set.

'*Mystery to Me* was probably the best Fleetwood Mac album since Peter Green had left the band three years earlier', Mick Fleetwood wrote in his 1990 autobiography, *Fleetwood: My Life and Adventures in Fleetwood Mac*. 'It was atmospheric and intelligent, and we knew it was going to be a big hit.'

Robert Christgau:

This album epitomizes what they've come to be, setting a gentle but evermore technological spaceyness over a bottom that, while never explosive, does drive the music with flair and economy: the least you can expect of a band named after its rhythm section. Even Bob Welch does himself proud.

With one of their best albums in the can, Fleetwood Mac once again headed to the US for a long tour. They were supported by acts such as Weather Report, Elvin Bishop, Rare Earth, Nazareth, The Strawbs, ZZ Top and Blue Oyster Cult.

Midnight Special

During the band's 1973 American tour, Fleetwood Mac appeared on the long-running NBC series, *The Midnight Special*, which aired weekly from 1973 to 1981. This rare footage of the short-lived but highly-regarded 1973 line-up – recorded on 19 October 1973 – sees Fleetwood Mac performing two songs from *Mystery to Me*: a steaming take on 'Miles Away' and a quite astonishing 'Believe Me', with Weston playing some very tasty guitar licks. Both performances are on YouTube and will be a revelation to anyone who hasn't paid attention to this era of Fleetwood Mac's career.

Au Revoir Bob Weston

Just as the band were beginning to gel particularly well in its live performances, Bob Weston was sacked. John McVie said that Bob was 'asked to leave after a disagreement'. The truth was more serious. Weston had started a clandestine relationship with his boss's wife. Or, as Samuel Graham put it, 'Bob Weston was lasciviously allied with Jenny Fleetwood'.

'Mick and his wife were having a bit of a domestic', Weston said. 'There was something unresolved. And there I was… and friendship developed into love.'

Mick Fleetwood in *Play On* in 2014:

It all stemmed from Jenny's need to connect and not getting what she needed from me. She was such a beguiling, beautiful creature that men were always smitten. In her mind, she valued the friendship and needed that connection, but it didn't always mean she wanted to get her knickers off. In the case of Weston, however, it did. It was horrible because Bob and I were good friends.

Weston said years later, still wistful; 'Jenny and I were born within an hour of each other. There was an empathy. We had an affair. Cost me a career that did'.

The band tried to put this setback behind them and continue with their itinerary, due to the legal and financial penalties that would be incurred if they cancelled. But after a gig at Lincoln, Nebraska, on 23 October 1973, Mick Fleetwood finally snapped, and, in Weston's absence, informed the rest of the band that he was no longer willing to work with him.

Weston recalled years later:

It was midway through an American tour. I had an early morning call from the tour manager, insisting I come up to his room, whereupon I was greeted with an air of hostility. My tour manager told me very simply that the tour was cancelled. Mick had already left for Africa, John and Christine for London – obviously, it was a *fait accompli*. Certainly, no mutual decision-making. I was handed a plane ticket and driven to the nearest airport. I didn't see any of the band between waking up and getting on the plane.

'I had taken off to Zambia', Mick Fleetwood says, 'because, to say the least, I needed to clear my head. The whole band did. Bob was fired, the tour was cancelled and everyone retreated to different parts of the world'. The remaining 26 dates of the tour were called off. They told Clifford Davis that they needed a break. Welch said:

'(We told him) we don't want to work until we say we want to work, and we don't want to make a record until we say we want to. The band's not breaking up, but we don't know what we want to do, and everybody just needs a long rest, so just wait until you hear from us'.

1974

Fakewood Mac

What happened next was one of the strangest stories of the 1970s.
Inconsistencies and anomalies surround the tale of the 'fake'
Fleetwood Mac.

With Weston's departure – and the autumn 1973 tour cut short – the
band went back to England to break the news to their manager Clifford
Davis.

At that time, it seems that Davis concluded that Fleetwood Mac had split
up for good. Clifford Davis:

> Mick Fleetwood came to my house with Christine (McVie) on 10 November
> 1973, to discuss the huge problem we had. I told him that we could just
> about get away with saying that he had had a nervous breakdown, but we
> simply 'had' to do the new set of 'make-up' dates within three months
> or we would be heavily sued and Fleetwood Mac would undoubtedly be
> finished for 'good'. (Christine) asked if I would finance (a solo album), and
> I said I would, providing I approved of the songs. So I was quite sure that
> 'she' wouldn't be in any future Fleetwood Mac line-up. I said to Mick, 'I do
> have some ideas. I've got a couple of lads I'm recording at present. I played
> him the tapes I'd recorded with them, which he liked a lot. So I arranged
> for Mick to meet these two guys.

Davis' understanding of the future of the current band was backed up by
the recollections of Fleetwood Mac's sound engineer, Robert Simon, who
told Bob Brunning that at a band meeting immediately after Bob Weston
was fired: 'the tour was over and Fleetwood Mac was breaking up. Bob
Welch seemed highly disgruntled with all that was taking place'.

Bob Welch:

> Clifford Davis sent me, Mick, John and Chris a letter, saying that he 'was
> not going down because of the whims of irresponsible musicians', after
> having 'pulled', what he called, 'every string and stroke in the book'. Davis
> also said, in that letter, that he intended to put together a 'star-quality,
> headlining act' and that he was offering us 'jobs' in this band, and we could
> take them, or not. I don't think that any of us responded to that letter. Be
> that as it may, Davis, without telling any of us, subsequent to that letter,
> booked the 'bogus' Fleetwood Mac on a US tour.

Davis: 'Mick told me he was off to Africa and to go ahead and organise auditions. We should 'rehearse the band up', and that he would come back a week before the departure date, rehearse with the band and then go on the tour'.

Keyboard player Dave Wilkinson: 'I got home and there was this telegram. And it was 'Top Secret! Get in touch with this number…''.

Wilkinson – who had spent six months in Christine McVie's old band, Chicken Shack, between July and December 1973 – was invited to an audition in King's Cross, London.

'Afterwards, we went to this little pub 'round the corner', he says. 'And Clifford Davis said to me 'you've got the job'. And I said, 'what job?''.

Davis also recruited singer Dave Terry (using the stage name Elmer Gantry, taken from a Sinclair Lewis novel about a hellfire preacher), guitarist Graham 'Kirby' Gregory from Curved Air, Paul Martinez on bass, and drummer, Craig Collinge. Gantry's remarkable physical resemblance to Bob Welch is presumably entirely coincidental.

Bob Welch: 'They were all English session musicians that Clifford had recruited. Pretty good too, just not Fleetwood Mac'.

The new band first met and rehearsed in mid-December 1973. According to Bob Brunning's account, roadie, Phil McDonnel, spoke individually with John McVie, Mick Fleetwood and Christine McVie over the next four weeks, and they all, tacitly or otherwise, approved of Davis' plan or at least did not explicitly disapprove. The credence to this scenario hangs on the intentions of Mick Fleetwood. Davis told the rest of the new band that Fleetwood would 'eventually' join with the rest of the musicians. The band's accountant, Dave Simmonds, signed an affidavit in April 1974, stating that this was his understanding also. Dave Walker – former Fleetwood Mac vocalist – concurred: 'Mick knew all about this "bogus" band', he has said.

In a 2017 BBC Radio interview, Gantry and Gregory confirmed they were told by Davis that they were forming the new Fleetwood Mac. But they alleged that Fleetwood's involvement in the project went much further than Fleetwood has since admitted. Gantry said, 'Mick Fleetwood came to our house and we talked through the new band, and it all seemed fine. Mick said, "well, I can't actually come and rehearse with you" – it was fairly imminent going to America to tour – "but if you get a (temporary) drummer, I'll join you for the tour"'.

Fleetwood denies all of this, and wrote in his second autobiography (2014): 'It was the most preposterous thing we had ever heard and the greatest betrayal from one of our own that we could have imagined'.

And yet, he had earlier said in the *Rock Family Trees* documentary (1995): 'I accept Clifford Davis' side of the story because I don't want to feel any other way'.

This new line-up of 'Fleetwood Mac' – without Mick Fleetwood or anyone else in the current or previous line-ups – was booked on a 40-date, three-month tour of the US. Well-known bands and singers such as Kiss, Nazareth, Status Quo, Tim Buckley and Rory Gallagher, were their support acts.

The tour opened in Pittsburgh on 16 January 1974. Bob Welch recalls: 'I was the one who first found out that Davis had been booking a fake Fleetwood Mac, after I happened to call a promoter named Rich Engler, who booked the Syrian Mosque in Pittsburgh, PA'.

As Engler tells it in his book *Behind the Stage Door*, he recalls seeing some unfamiliar British musicians arrive at the venue. When he asked Clifford Davis where Fleetwood Mac were, he was told they had just walked by. Having worked with Fleetwood Mac before, Engler expected to see at least a Fleetwood and a McVie or two.

'It was a nightmare', Engler wrote. '(But) they were actually really good. I don't know if the crowd was just really stoned or didn't know what Fleetwood Mac looked like.'

A week later, the *Pittsburgh Post-Gazette* ran a piece headlined 'Hey, What's Going on Here, Mac?', that recounted Engler's Fleetwood Mac embarrassment and included a statement from band management that Mick Fleetwood was ill and would be joining the tour when he recovered. According to Phil McDonnel, Mick Fleetwood was due to join the band at their third gig, at the Civic Center in Baltimore on 23 January 1974.

'I phoned Mick', he said, 'asking whether he was ready to come over. He replied that he was not, and still had a lot of personal matters to clear up'.

McDonnel spoke to Davis, who was back in the UK. Davis phoned Fleetwood.

'I asked him which flight he was going to be on', Davis recalled. 'And he said 'John's with me and I can't talk right now''.'

'I remember being at Benifold', says John McVie, 'with Bob and Mick. We'd got word that there was a fake Fleetwood Mac on the road'.

And, ten minutes later, according to Davis, he had a call from his lawyer.

Meanwhile, five hapless musicians needed to fulfil eight weeks of bookings.

'The first gig went down a storm', Dave Wilkinson said. 'It wasn't a bad band. We performed those old Fleetwood Mac numbers quite well.

We thought everything was going to be alright, although a few questions were asked.'

The fifth date was scheduled for the Academy of Music, New York City, on 26 January 1974.

'I'd heard conversations and saw long faces', Wilkinson recalled. 'And it was finally confirmed that Mick Fleetwood would not be going to come out. The news was beginning to spread that this wasn't the 'real' Fleetwood Mac. Everyone was getting worried. It was quite frightening, really.'

Clifford Davis – by then present in the US – went on stage to address a restless audience.

'Don't worry', he shouted, 'I 'am' Fleetwood Mac!'.

Dave Wilkinson: 'I just accepted the whole thing philosophically… 'I'm getting paid', I thought, 'I'm enjoying myself!'".

It Was A Hard Week For Fleetwood Mac

Fleetwood Mac, the British rock-blues group, had a hard time of it Saturday at the Academy of Music on 14th Street when it started its current American tour. Last week, the group's drummer quit and was hurriedly replaced, and on Saturday, the lead singer came down with laryngitis. A packed audience waited with surprising patience until a to-play-or-not-play decision was made – Fleetwood Mac agreed to perform an instrumental set without the ailing singer. It was simple rolling rock, most of it based firmly on the blues form. Offers of refunds were made, but most of the audience stayed on. Fleetwood Mac has completely changed personnel since its last New York visit, but not its approach to the music. (Support band) Silverhead, because of the Fleetwood Mac crisis, was forced to extend its playing to nearly 90 minutes. This was not to the advantage of the British group, which found its basic rock style stretched a little thin.

(*New York Times*, 28 January 1974)

The tour progressed to Los Angeles, Denver, Long Beach, San Jose and Salt Lake City before grinding to a halt on 20 February 1974 in Edmonton, Alabama, as news of the bogus band became public knowledge.

'People were just shouting (at us) all the time', Dave Wilkinson said. ''Get off, where's the real Fleetwood Mac?''

Rolling Stone discussed the tour at length in its 28 February issue, reproduced here in full.

When is a Fleetwood Mac not a Fleetwood Mac? Although there is a band called Fleetwood Mac currently in the midst of a two-and-a-half-month US tour, that question is puzzling some promoters, some fans and Warner Bros. – all of whom thought Fleetwood Mac was Mick Fleetwood (drums), Bob Welch (guitar, vocals), John McVie (bass), Christine McVie (vocals, keyboards) and Bob Weston (vocals, guitar).

About the only person who isn't pondering the question is Clifford Davis, manager of Fleetwood Mac. In the dressing room at Howard Stein's Academy of Music, where the band was to play their seventh gig on the tour on January 26th – Davis introduced a band which did not have one member of the Fleetwood Mac last seen or heard on tour or album.

'I want to get this out of the public's mind as far as the band being Mick Fleetwood's band,' said Davis. 'This band is my band. This band has always been my band.'

The band Davis has on the road now is composed of musicians named Elmer Gantry (lead singer), Kirby (guitar), Paul Martinez (bass), David Wilkinson (piano) and Craig Collinge (drums). The drummer, according to Davis, substituted at the last moment for Mick Fleetwood on this tour. It was at the end of the last tour in August, said Davis, that 'I just decided it was time to change the band, certainly onstage, and that's what I did. I've always been sort of the leader. I've always sort of picked who was going to be in it and who wasn't. I decided to keep Mick.'

But, Davis claimed, trouble at home forced Mick to fly right back to England the day after he arrived in America on January 13th, so Davis quickly flew over Craig, a friend of the other musicians, to fill in. Davis said that before each show, he is informing the audience that Mick had personal problems and had to return home. However, informed sources say that Fleetwood was never booked to fly to America and that he did not come to the States at all. Bob Welch, the American guitarist who joined Fleetwood two and a half years ago when original member Jeremy Spencer found God in Los Angeles, denied the whole Davis story, and at presstime was en route to England to meet with Fleetwood, the McVies, Weston and lawyers, to straighten the whole matter out.

Said Welch on the phone before he left California: 'It is a rip-off. The manager put together a group real fast using the name Fleetwood Mac before we had a chance to do anything about it.'

According to Welch, the band stopped touring last October because Mick was in the process of getting a divorce and they all needed a rest. While the band was in various countries on vacation, Welch said, 'We all got letters from Clifford Davis indicating his intentions to put a new band back on the road. He issued an ultimatum to all of us. In effect, what happened was that we got offered gigs, which is not really his place to do.

'We said, "Well, hell, we're not going to do that. We want to go back on the road in such-and-such length of time." Nobody accepted the offer, and so the guy proceeded to get together another band, and he worked with ATI, the agency, and they went out to grab the big bucks.'

Fleetwood Mac's agent, Bruce Payne, denied the story, ascribing it to the original group's 'bitterness.' He backed up Davis' story about Mick Fleetwood's sudden departure.

At Warner Bros. in Burbank, Don Schmitzerle, executive director, label management, has been on the case. 'I'm in the midst of trying to find out who has exclusivity on the name,' he said. Until then, the record company can do nothing.

'To the band's thinking,' said Welch, 'that's kind of beside the point. If he (Davis) has the rights to the band's name, theoretically he can put anybody there. He can put four dogs barking on a leash and call it Fleetwood Mac. '

Davis, who has been Fleetwood's manager from the start in 1967, emphasizes time and again, 'I've always been the leader of the band as such. A lot of people over the years have misconstrued the Fleetwood Mac as Fleetwood and McVie. "Fleetwood Mac" was a song written by Peter Green when he was with John Mayall.' In fact, Davis points out, McVie was not the group's first bass player, but a guy named Bob Brunning was, and so, technically, Mick Fleetwood is the only original member left.

Davis' troubles started at the first date in Pittsburgh, when promoter Rich Engler discovered that the Fleetwood Mac who had arrived for the gig was not the group he knew. Engler and his partner complained to the manager, to no avail. No announcement was made of the changes, but as soon as they began to play, about a dozen Fleetwood fans demanded refunds. Engler and partner Pat DiCesare gave the money back when Davis refused.

By the time Howard Stein heard about the new Fleetwood Mac, the Academy was already nearly sold out. When Stein had presented The Byrds at the Academy, he knew in advance they were all new musicians and in his ads, he listed each musician's name to inform the public. But in the case of Fleetwood Mac, there wasn't enough time, so he arranged for Davis to make an announcement before the show that there would be all new musicians in the band and that Mick Fleetwood couldn't make it. Stein was going to offer refunds to anyone not satisfied.

But a half hour before they were scheduled to go on, it seemed that the vocalist Elmer had lost his voice.

'This has never happened to me before,' Elmer said in a raspy voice. He claimed that he had been trying all day to hit notes, but he just couldn't do it.

Frantic huddles took place between Davis, Payne, house manager Terry Holmes and Stein's assistant Jane Rose. Stein himself was in Miami promoting another show. It seems Elmer had performed without any difficulties the night before in Potsdam, New York, but on the day of the Academy gig – one, incidentally, where the press would be watching this Fleetwood Mac – he had come down with a bad throat. Elmer had no idea when it would get better. The doctor had told him it was inflamed and given him antibiotics. But, no one had told the Academy promoters about this until the band actually arrived at the house in the middle of the second band's set. Not only had this situation never arisen before at the Academy, but the usual practice in case of illness is for the band to inform the promoter before the show. Had the promoter known even an hour before showtime, the entire show could have been cancelled and all tickets refunded.

While discussions raged in the office, most of the 3,400 people in the house listened to records and sat passively watching as all equipment was cleared from the stage. Finally, Davis and Payne decided to put the band on without a vocalist just to jam. Stein reportedly convinced them by phone that if they didn't go on at all, there'd be a real crowd problem. The audience had already sat through Kiss and Silverhead.

And so Holmes made the announcement that Mick Fleetwood had personal problems and left for England and that the singer had lost his voice. The band would still jam, but anyone who wasn't satisfied could leave within the next fifteen minutes and get a refund. A few boos greeted the announcement, a few cries of 'Fleetwood Mac' penetrated the air, but most of the audience stayed and listened to a half-hour of some basic boogie jamming. Only about 800 people asked for refunds. A few minutes after midnight, Davis took the microphone and told the audience, 'We're going to try to work out something with the promoter to come back in March.'

But by March, Fleetwood Mac could be a whole other cast of characters. Before Bob Welch flew off to England to rejoin his colleagues and meet with lawyers, he left word: 'The tide seems to be turning.'

'We were all on holiday when we found out what had happened', **Fleetwood told *Rolling Stone* later that year. 'Before the bogus band**

played too many dates, we had to physically get together and take legal advice. The impression Clifford had given was that he had every legal right to do what he did. We very soon found out, apart from morally having no excuse, there was no legal right.'

'We would sit around the table at Benifold for hours debating what to do', Fleetwood wrote later. 'The first thing we had to do was file a lawsuit against Davis. We had no idea how far Clifford would take his pursuit of ownership.'

Bob Welch reflected years later:

The Clifford Davis lawsuit was probably the most difficult time Fleetwood Mac ever had to go through. We got an injunction to stop the bogus band in England, which took a couple months to obtain through the English courts. All this time, myself and Mick were calling long-distance to L.A. to talk to Mo Ostin at Warners. I took on the job of rallying Mick, John and Chris to the idea that we had to fight this, or forever forget about Fleetwood Mac. There was some reluctance. Christine was (even back then) tired of going on the road, and had talked about wanting to 'retire' and run a small shop or something. There was a feeling that maybe Fleetwood Mac was over with anyway, since everybody knew that the most successful line-up since the Pete Green band was the *Mystery* line up with me and Bob Weston. If we had been able to continue to tour with that band – instead of cancelling a third of the way through – *Mystery to Me* probably would have 'gone platinum' that same year.

'When things like this have happened', Fleetwood said in 1974, 'many bands haven't had the stamina to see it through. It's very easy to say, 'God, it's just not worth it'. I'm sure Clifford never felt for one moment that we would stick this out. We manage ourselves now'.

'The Clifford Davis thing was settled out of court, after much agony (and money paid to lawyers) on both sides', Bob Welch recalled in 1999. It was October 1976 before terms were agreed. Gantry and Kirby, meanwhile, returned to London and formed the band Stretch. Their bitter song about the saga – a terrific slab of 1970s white funk called 'Why Did You Do It?' – reached the UK top 20 in late 1975. In an odd twist of fate, bassist Paul Martinez would join Cristine McVie's old band, Chicken Shack, in 1976. Much later, he would work with Robert Plant and be part of the Led Zeppelin reunion at Live Aid.

Los Angeles Calling...

The aftermath of the fake band's tour was that the credibility of the genuine Fleetwood Mac was now suspect. And so Mick Fleetwood, John McVie, Christine McVie and Bob Welch had to start again. Bob Welch:

> The most difficult thing was to convince Warner Bros records to let us record another album. They at first didn't want to, because they feared that the court might decide that Clifford Davis really did 'own' the name Fleetwood Mac, in which case Warners would have been in deep, you know what. It became obvious that if we were going to be successful in convincing Warners before there was a formal court judgment – which might take years – that we would have to physically move to L.A., where the head office was located. I began to talk to Mick about relocating. Nobody wanted to do this except me. Over the course of the next month or two, I kept pushing Mick, who by then was 100% convinced. He kept bringing it up with Chris, and gradually the decision was made to move the band, roadies and all.

Fleetwood and the McVies agreed to a six-month sojourn in California. 'We were going to Los Angeles', said Mick Fleetwood, 'to regroup and start again, or fail trying'.

Heroes are Hard to Find

Personnel:
Mick Fleetwood: drums, percussion
Christine McVie: keyboards, vocals, ARP String Ensemble
John McVie: bass guitar
Bob Welch: guitar, vocals, vibraphone
with
Sneaky Pete Kleinow: pedal steel guitar on 'Come A Little Bit Closer'
Recorded at Angel City Sound, Los Angeles, July 1974.
Produced by Fleetwood Mac.
Album release: 13 September 1974.
Highest chart placings: UK: did not chart US: 34
Side one: 'Heroes Are Hard To Find', 'Coming Home', 'Angel', 'Bermuda Triangle', 'Come A Little Bit Closer'
Side two: 'She's Changing Me', 'Bad Loser', 'Silver Heels', 'Prove Your Love', 'Born Enchanter', 'Safe Harbour'

'Heroes Are Hard To Find' b/w 'Born Enchanter'

US Single release: February 1975 (did not chart).
The single edit of 'Heroes Are Hard To Find' is available on 50 Years – Don't Stop.

The proof that their formula has finally trapped them is the pitifulness of their attempts to escape – with string synthesizer, pedal steel, half-assed horns, and other catch-22s of the International Pop Music Community. Bob Welch sounds bored, which is certainly poetic justice, and even Christine McVie is less than perfect this time out. Their worst.
(Robert Christgau, *Village Voice*, 1974)

'We landed in Los Angeles in the spring of 1974', Mick Fleetwood recalls. 'What was meant to be a six-month trip turned into a two-and-a-half-year legal battle and a permanent relocation.'
Says John McVie:

In my opinion, it was the best thing we ever did. America had always been the place where you had to go to really 'make it'. I'd grown up listening to American music, and anything that came out of America – with a few exceptions – was okay with me. We'd been very successful in Europe, and then not so successful, and there didn't seem like there was any way to 'break out' other than by actually living (in the US) and working the circuit. The only regrets I had were that my family and relatives were so far away, back in Europe.

But whilst they were able to stop the fake Fleetwood Mac from performing, Davis in turn was able to stop the 'real' Fleetwood Mac from giving concerts until the dispute had been settled. Their royalties were also tied up, putting the band under great financial pressure. Unable to tour, but supported by Warner Brothers, they returned to the studio. The album *Heroes are Hard to Find* was recorded at Angel City Sound in Los Angeles in July 1974. It's a decent album, but a step down from *Mystery to Me*. It's hardly surprising that they had less conviction this time around. Despite this, the momentum from *Mystery to Me* and their unrelenting touring schedule over the previous few years ensured that *Heroes are Hard to Find* was Fleetwood Mac's highest-charting album in the US: their first top 40 album.
'It was the first time we'd ever had one guitarist, and I don't think it would have worked before then', Fleetwood recalled, 'but Bob Welch delivered. It made me reconsider what Fleetwood Mac meant

and what was possible. The album didn't chart in England, but we didn't care'.

Heroes are Hard to Find is very much Bob Welch's album – he wrote all but four songs. But it's two of Christine McVie's contributions which have stood the test of time and point directly to the massive success that the band would soon enjoy.

The horn-driven opening title track is pleasant and sounds great with lovely harmonies but lacks inspiration – it ambles past mostly on two chords. Likewise, 'Bad Loser' has an attractive samba rhythm, but an underdeveloped melody. Bob Welch: "Bad Loser' was about Clifford Davis. Mick did the kind of beat to it, however, that he didn't usually do on her pop songs'.

'Prove Your Love', though, is an exquisitely pretty mid-tempo ballad with a simple heartfelt chorus. Christine McVie is in wonderful voice here. Better still, the magnificent, majestic 'Come A Little Bit Closer' is the album's *bona fide* classic, with Chris McVie's expressive piano and vocals and surging orchestral strings, sweetened by Sneaky Pete Kleinow's pedal steel guitar. Bob Welch: "Come A Little Bit Closer' should have been a hit single, in my opinion'.

Listen to this and then to Joan Armatrading's 'Love And Affection': two peas from the same pod.

Bob Welch, for all his talent, is stretched a little thinly on *Heroes are Hard to Find* as songwriter, joint lead singer and sole guitarist. There's nothing to match 'Hypnotised', 'Sentimental Lady' or 'Future Games' here.

'Bermuda Triangle', his best song on the album, is ominous and perhaps overambitious – it's a long song, pretentious in places, a little introspective and over-earnest.

You're feeling safe in your harbour
And everything seems certain
Right next to Palm Beach and Key Biscane
Behind a velvet curtain
But then the moon goes grey with worry
And the sea turns a pale white
You better believe something strange is going on tonight

Bob Welch:

'Bermuda Triangle' started as a drum track to some song – I forget which – that wasn't exactly working. So, I asked the engineer to speed up Mick's drum track by 20-25%, and then I wrote a new song to that. Sometimes happy songs can sound sad, and vice versa, if you mess with 'em enough.

'Born Enchanter' hits a silky groove but doesn't hook in the listener. 'Angel' has a swampy rhythm sticking rigidly to two chords. It's not the song recorded four years later for *Tusk*. 'Coming Home' is pure Bob Welch: a mellow, jazz-tinged, trippy tune drifting past without ever grabbing the listener. His trademark octave guitars hark back to the spacey vibe of Hendrix' 'Third Stone From The Sun'. The uplifting 'She's Changing Me' is lightweight pop-rock in the ELO vein, and all the better for that. 'Silver Heels' has a tough lead vocal and gorgeous production with some nice guitar licks. For reasons best known to Welch himself, a rewrite of 'Silver Heels' – re-titled 'The Hustler', with explicit lyrics – appeared on *Bob Welch Looks at Bop* (1999).

The album closes with an atmospheric instrumental called 'Safe Harbour', which ebbs and flows and cops most of its feel from 'Albatross'.

Not surprisingly, given the events of the previous few months, *Heroes are Hard to Find* lacks many of the qualities of Fleetwood Mac's previous three albums: *Future Games*, *Penguin* and *Mystery to Me*. What's most important is the *sound* of the album – radio-friendly, firmly within the West Coast vibe. Much of this should be credited to Bob Welch, although his idiosyncrasies would need to be smoothed by Buckingham and Nicks before major success would finally knock on Fleetwood Mac's door.

Heroes are Hard to Find Tour

Fleetwood Mac started a nine-week, 43-date American tour on 29 September 1974 at the John Long Centre, Scranton, PA.

The setlist comprised highlights from *Heroes are Hard to Find*, the best of the previous four albums, and some classics. Bob Welch performed the title track from *Future Games*, 'Sentimental Lady' from *Bare Trees*, 'Night Watch' from *Penguin*, 'Hypnotised' from *Mystery to Me*, and three new songs from *Heroes are Hard to Find*: 'Coming Home', 'Bermuda Triangle' and 'Angel'. Chris McVie's songs were 'Spare Me A Little of Your Love' and 'Homeward Bound' from *Bare Trees*, 'Why?' from *Mystery to Me* and 'Bad Loser' from *Heroes are Hard to Find*. From the band's back catalogue, 'I'd Rather Go Blind', 'The Green Manalishi (With The Two Prong Crown)', 'Oh Well' and 'Rattlesnake Shake' rounded out a terrific set of songs.

Fleetwood Mac took a second keyboard player with them for this tour. For the first two weeks, they were supplemented by Doug Graves, playing organ and string synthesiser. Graves was replaced by Bobby Hunt for the rest of the tour.

Bob Welch: 'Bobby Hunt, on keyboards, was my old friend from The Seven Souls. The late Doug Graves was an engineer during the *Heroes Are Hard to Find* record(ing sessions)'.

Fleetwood Mac were supported on the tour by the German progressive rock band, Triumvirat, who played the whole of their new album *Illusions on a Double Dimple*.

The Ultrasonic Broadcast

WLIR was a popular progressive rock radio station based out of Hempstead, on the eastern edge of New York City. The station hosted and broadcast a long-running series of live concerts from the nearby Ultrasonic Recording Studios. Artists featured included Bruce Springsteen, The Allman Brothers Band, Dr. John, Jackson Browne, The Doobie Brothers, Billy Joel, Hall & Oates and many other notable performers of the era. Fleetwood Mac performed a 70-minute, eleven-song set on 8 October 1974. Bob Welch's voice may be ragged, but his guitar playing is inspired. It's unthinkable that this has never been officially released.

Setlist: 'The Green Manalishi', 'Spare Me A Little Of Your Love', 'Sentimental Lady', 'Future Games', 'Bermuda Triangle', 'Why?', 'Angel', 'Homeward Bound', 'Rattlesnake Shake', 'Hypnotised', 'Black Magic Woman'.

Don Kirshner's Rock Concert

Don Kirshner's Rock Concert premiered for the first time on broadcast television in 1973. Every Saturday night at 11.30 p.m., rock fans were able to see sets by such well-known acts as The Allman Brothers Band, Bad Company, Badfinger, Black Sabbath, David Bowie, Alice Cooper, The Eagles, Pat Benatar, The Doobie Brothers, Edgar Winter, Rory Gallagher, George Harrison, Billy Joel, Journey, KISS, Lynyrd Skynyrd, Rush, The Ramones, Steve Miller, Van Morrison and many more. It's an invaluable trove of classic rock performances.

The 14 December 1974 episode (Season 2, Episode 13) featured Blue Swede, Weather Report and Fleetwood Mac. Fleetwood Mac performed 'The Green Manalishi (With The Two Prong Crown)', 'Spare Me A Little Of Your Love', 'Bermuda Triangle', 'Rattlesnake Shake', 'Shake Your Moneymaker' and 'Black Magic Woman'. It's a tight performance and fascinating to watch.

KSAN Broadcast

In mid-December, Fleetwood Mac recorded a session at the Record Plant, Sausalito, for broadcast on KSAN: a popular free format radio station in the Bay Area of San Francisco. Bob Welch's performance is quite superb: he doesn't sound like someone on the verge of quitting the band. Eight weeks of live dates as the band's sole guitar player had really improved his playing.

The setlist kicks off with a tight rendition of 'The Green Manalishi (With The Two Prong Crown)', and runs through wonderful versions of 'Angel', 'Spare Me A Little Of Your Love', 'Sentimental Lady', 'Future Games', 'Bermuda Triangle', 'Why?', 'Believe Me', 'Black Magic Woman', 'Oh Well', 'Rattlesnake Shake' and 'Hypnotised'. The entire show was released in 2020 on the *1969 to 1974* box set.

Bob Welch Departs

By 31 December 1974 – exactly halfway through the 1970s – Fleetwood Mac had worked through eight (or nine, or ten) line-ups in the previous five years. Seemingly in a state of permanent flux, the next change in personnel was, more or less, a fluke. During a break in the band's touring a few weeks before the end of the year – either in the second week of November or in early December – Mick Fleetwood went shopping:

I'd driven my Caddy down the winding road to the Canyon Country Store to buy some groceries. I ran into a guy who I knew from the scene around town (Thomas Christian) who was doing some PR work for a new recording studio, inviting musicians he knew to come and check it out. It was called Sound City.

They chatted, and Fleetwood, acting on instinct again, immediately agreed to visit the studio in Van Nuys, about twenty-minutes-drive from Laurel Canyon. Thus are fortunes made. Mick Fleetwood:

Sound City was fine: the live room seemed like it could capture drums well, and when I met the house engineer Keith Olsen, I liked him a lot. I thought it could be the perfect place to record our next album.

Keith Olsen:

Mick was introduced to me by an acquaintance of mine. His name escapes me. We made plans to talk further about me producing the next album by

Mac. When he came out to Sound City, we made a deal for me to produce the next album in February of the next year. I played several things that I had done at the studio.

Olsen offered to play them some music that had been recorded at Sound City the year before: a track by the duo Buckingham Nicks, who were, coincidentally, recording overdubs in an adjacent studio.

Olsen first heard Nicks and Buckingham perform with Bay Area psych-rock band, Fritz, initially formed in 1966 at high school and known as the Fritz Rabyne Memorial Band. Fritz's management had tried unsuccessfully to get A and B-list record producers to give them a listen. They moved onto 'all the C and C-minus list producers', Olsen says now. 'I was in that category and heard a little demo and I said, 'Sure I'll go up and see them. A free trip to the Bay Area, see a band and come home'. I was picked up by Lindsey and I think, the drummer in the band van, and I was thrown in the back in between a bunch of amps and drum cases. And then I was asked to carry the stuff in with them and help them set up.'

Olsen invited Fritz to Sound City to record. Buckingham had been focusing on playing bass, but he developed a distinctive acoustic guitar style while recuperating from mononucleosis.

Olsen explains:

The guitar sounds different when you hit it with the back of your fingers instead of the pick. And also during that time, Lindsey started recording some ideas on this little four-track machine he had: all these songs he and Stevie wrote that are on the *Buckingham Nicks* album. He brought them down one day and played them for me and I said, 'Holy crap. Let's do this album'.

Buckingham Nicks was released in September 1973 but bombed, despite the presence of some first-rate LA session musicians such as Waddy Wachtel, Jerry Scheff and Jim Keltner. A year later, they had been dropped by their record label and moved in with Olsen.

'Our record company had no idea what to do with us', Buckingham later complained in *Rolling Stone*. 'They said something about wanting us to be the new Jim Stafford (a country-pop novelty act), and they wanted us to play steakhouses.'

Richie Unterberger said in *Fleetwood Mac: The Complete Illustrated History*:

Nicks worked as a Hollywood waitress and had cleaned Olsen's home for cash when funds were especially low. At other low points, Buckingham had even sold ads over the phone, resorting to writing bad checks for meals at Hollywood coffee shops. Nicks' parents offered to support her, but only if she moved back to their home and went back to school – a deal that must have seemed tempting as the pair slid into near-poverty.

And then, by chance, Mick Fleetwood entered the picture.

'Keith cued up 'Frozen Love', the last track on their album', Fleetwood recalled. 'Seven enchanting minutes of vocal harmony and dynamic guitar.'

'He was standing there grooving to this searing guitar solo', Lindsey Buckingham recalls, 'and he needed a guitar player. That was as far as his thinking went. Mick had not only bought into Keith's engineering but also into my guitar playing.

'Mick came back and said that he'd found this fantastic guitar player', says Christine McVie. 'It was really only a guitar player that we were interested in.'

Bob Welch:

Mick had gone out to check out studios to do the next album after *Heroes* ... while I was still hemming and hawing. I hemmed and hawed for months about whether or not I would leave Fleetwood Mac. At Sound City studios, somebody played him a tape of Stevie and Lindsey. Mick told me about hearing their tape and how good they were, that he had heard these great singers and writers at Sound City. (This was) before I had officially left the band. At that point, I could've chosen to stay in Fleetwood Mac and add Stevie and Lindsey to the line-up. It wasn't like anybody was asking me to leave, and there was a moment that I thought about staying.

Shortly afterwards, however, Welch handed in his notice. His last formal appearance with Fleetwood Mac was on 15 December 1974: the Record Plant radio session. Subsequent events suggest that he resigned just after Christmas.

'Bob just quit', John McVie remembered, 'I'll never know why'.

Welch said twenty-five years later:

John McVie told me, 'Bob, it'll be the biggest mistake you'll ever make'. Everybody knew that we had to find some new creative 'juice'. I left Fleetwood Mac mainly because I felt like it was time to 'risk it' and see what I could do on my own. I felt the band had reached a sort of dead end creatively. I got my record deal at Capitol based on the strength of *Future Games* through *Heroes* ... I don't know exactly what day I left. I basically finished out the tour about late December 1974.

'Bob's exit wasn't like the others', Mick Fleetwood wrote later. 'There was no big blow-up, no signs it was coming, no change in his character, and no hard feelings. It was all above board and, to me, all the more a sad goodbye.'

Fleetwood had clearly forgotten about Welch suing him in 1994 for breach of contract related to underpayment of royalties. Coincidentally, or otherwise, Welch was not inducted to the Rock and Roll Hall of Fame in 1998 with eight other members of Fleetwood Mac. Bob Welch:

It seems to me that Mick treats most past band members as if they didn't really have anything to do with Fleetwood Mac, with the exception of the *Rumours* band, Peter Green, and rarely, Jeremy Spencer. Everybody else who ever played with him he 'shuts out of his mind', kinda like in the old Soviet Union, where they used to 'erase' politicians from official histories and never mention them in public. Mick is very lucky in that his last name just happens to be the name of the band. If Mick's last name had been 'Jones' or 'Smith', he would have never been able to get away with the heavy-handed tactics he has used with former band members.

Bob Welch was an intelligent man and a fine musician. His contribution to Fleetwood Mac's five albums over almost four years between April 1971 and December 1974 should not be underestimated. He wrote or co-wrote two-thirds of the 23 songs on *Mystery to Me* and *Heroes are Hard to Find*.

'My era was the bridge era', Welch told the Cleveland newspaper, *The Plain Dealer*, in 1998. 'It was a transition. But it was an important period in the history of the band.'

Welch had considerable success as a solo artist in the 1970s, including a re-recording of 'Sentimental Lady' with members of Fleetwood Mac. Bob Welch died on 7 June 2012, by his own hand at his home in Nashville, weary of acute pain from a botched medical procedure. 'He was a huge part of our history which sometimes gets forgotten', Mick Fleetwood said in a statement at the time. 'If you look into our musical history, you'll see a huge period that was completely ensconced in Bob's work.'

After Bob Welch quit, 'we were in panic mode once more', Fleetwood says in his memoirs. 'I called Keith Olsen. 'Bob Welch has left us, so we're looking for a new guitar player. I was calling about that guy who's playing I heard in your studio. I'd like to ask him to join our band''.

Fleetwood called Olsen on New Year's Eve, 31 December 1974.

Keith Olsen: 'And Mick said, 'You know those two kids you played for me? You think they'd want to join my band?'. So I said, 'I don't know, but I can ask them'. He said, 'Could you do it tonight?'. They were getting ready to have a party and I said, 'We have something to talk about'.

Lindsey Buckingham: 'We were having a New Year's party at our house… wondering if 1975 would be a better year for us. And Keith walked in and said, 'Hey, I've got some news'. You could have knocked me down with a feather. I had to explain we came as a duo. Stupid me, eh?'.

Stevie Nicks: 'Nobody, unless he was totally crazy, would try and sell someone not only on a guitar player, but a girl singer, too. Maybe one of us, but not the twin set'.

'And so from about eight o'clock to about two in the morning', Olsen says, 'I sat upstairs and tried to convince them to join Fleetwood Mac'.

'The night that Keith told us that Mick might ask us to join', Buckingham says, 'this friend of ours who was really into Fleetwood Mac was there. He told us about seeing them at Winterland and how they'd driven away in big black Cadillac limousines. Even without knowing much about them, I was awestruck'.

'I convinced them to just go and work with them for, say, four weeks, and see how you fit in', recalls Keith Olsen.

Buckingham and Nicks met Fleetwood and the McVies the following evening at a Mexican restaurant – the *El Carmen* – on West 3rd Street in Los Angeles.

'As soon as we all met together, there was a definite rapport', Buckingham said. And as Mick Fleetwood wrote in his memoirs:

I knew I wanted Lindsey and Stevie in Fleetwood Mac, but the decision wasn't all mine. We wanted to make sure that Chris was fine with (another woman joining the band). Chris and Stevie hit it off straight away.

'Lindsey, Stevie, can I ask you something?' I said. Everyone else stopped talking and looked at me. I shot looks at John and Chris to make sure I wasn't out of line, and I wasn't.

'So, would you like to join our band?'

They turned to each other for a moment, beamed and said 'Yes'.

Life changing moments can be that simple.

1975

A New Age
Stevie Nicks told *Billboard.com* in 2013:

Lindsey and I were breaking up when Fleetwood Mac asked us to join. We moved down from San Francisco to L.A. in 1972, and made Buckingham Nicks in 1973, and were having problems all through that. When we moved, it was lonely. I didn't have any girlfriends. And I was the one who worked. I had to be a waitress, and a cleaning lady, in order to support us, because Lindsey didn't want to play four sets at Chuck's Steakhouse, where we could've made $500 a week. To him, that was selling out. He wanted to play original music, so I went along with that. When we joined Fleetwood Mac, I said, 'Okay, this is what we've been working for since 1968. And so Lindsey, you and I have to sew this relationship back up. We have too much to lose here. We need to put our problems behind us. Maybe we're not going to have any more problems, because we're finally going to have some money. And I won't have to be a waitress'. If we hadn't joined Fleetwood Mac, would Lindsey and I have carried on and made it? I was really tired of having no money and being a waitress. It's very possible that I would have gone back to school and Lindsey would have gone back to San Francisco. Lindsey and I were in total chaos a year before we met Fleetwood Mac. I had already moved out of our apartment a couple of times and then had to move back in because I couldn't afford it. Our relationship was already in dire straits. But if we'd broken up within the first six months of Fleetwood Mac, there would have been no record and we would have been in big trouble, so when we joined the band, we took the decision to hang in there. I made Lindsey listen to all the Fleetwood Mac records. And I said, 'I think we can do something for this band. We'll do it for a year, save some money and if we don't like it, we'll quit'. And he's like, 'But *Buckingham Nicks*, I still think the record's going to start to break out'. I said, 'You wait around. I'm sick of being a waitress. We are joining Fleetwood Mac and we're going to be great'. I got an apartment on Hollywood Boulevard, he moved back in with me, and we kind of put our relationship back together. We weren't fighting about money, we had a really nice place, and we were going to work with these hysterically funny English people every day, making great music.

'John and Mick', Lindsey Buckingham said in 1977, 'have always been open to having a lot of different people in the band – which is odd. I would never be able to do that. I would think it was real important to keep an identity. I remember being a kid – if a new member joined a group, I just didn't like that at all. But that openness is what's kept them going for so long'.

John McVie: 'By the time we met Stevie and Lindsey, the band had pretty much moved away from its beginnings as a pure blues band. In fact, you could say that had started with 'Albatross' and 'Man Of The World'. So when Stevie and Lindsey joined, it wasn't a big shock. I was as sold as Mick was when I heard them'.

Mick Fleetwood: 'We hired Stevie and Lindsey as salaried members of Fleetwood Mac, paying them $200 a week. Chris returned home to see her family, while John, Lindsey and I, began rehearsing in a garage we rented in Santa Monica'.

Christine McVie returned to the US, and the new five-piece Fleetwood Mac performed together for the first time in the basement of their agent's offices. The first song they rehearsed was one of Christine's: 'Say You Love Me'. The song would open side two of *Fleetwood Mac* and be the opening number at every Fleetwood Mac live show for the next five years.

John McVie: '(At) the first rehearsal in the basement of our agent … I heard Chris, Lindsey and Stevie singing together, doing a 'three part' for the first time. Very exciting! Lindsey's playing blew me away. Stevie's voice and songs. You could say I was impressed!'.

Christine McVie: 'I started playing 'Say You Love Me' … and fell right into it. I heard this incredible sound – our three voices – and said to myself, 'Is this me singing?'. I couldn't believe how great this three-voice harmony was. My skin turned to goose flesh, and I wondered how long this feeling was going to last'.

'It all seemed to come together very quickly', Lindsey Buckingham said. 'Certainly, the vocal blend was very important.'

Mick Fleetwood: 'It was so natural and so powerful when they harmonised, that I could barely keep playing. The three of them became one voice'.

That there was a large measure of luck in the recruitment of Buckingham and Nicks is without doubt. Or perhaps it was fate. Either way, for Lindsey Buckingham – insecure and egotistic but massively talented and with a very clear vision – seven years of hustling as a jobbing musician were about to end. A consummate craftsman – very different to Welch, Weston and Kirwan (and Green and Spencer) before him – Buckingham not only provided commercial songs of his own, but also an

ear for a melody and sackful of ideas for how to embellish the songs of his
bandmates. His high harmonies sailed above Christine McVie at the low
end and Stevie Nicks in the middle: a combination of voices that worked
commercially and artistically. It's no coincidence that the two albums the
band recorded without him – *Behind the Mask* (1990) and *Time* (1995) –
suffer greatly from his absence.

Fleetwood Mac

Personnel:
Lindsey Buckingham: electric, acoustic and resonator guitar, banjo, vocals
Mick Fleetwood: drums, percussion
Christine McVie: keyboards, synthesizer, vocals
John McVie: bass guitar
Stevie Nicks: vocals
with
Waddy Wachtel: rhythm guitar on 'Sugar Daddy'
Recorded at Sound City Studios, Van Nuys, California, January-February 1975.
Produced by Fleetwood Mac and Keith Olsen.
Album release: 11 July 1975.
Highest chart placings: UK; 23, US: 1
Side one: 'Monday Morning', 'Warm Ways', 'Blue Letter', 'Rhiannon', 'Over My
Head', 'Crystal'
Side two: 'Say You Love Me', 'Landslide', 'World Turning', 'Sugar Daddy', 'I'm So Afraid'

'Over My Head' b/w 'I'm So Afraid'
US single release: 24 September 1975 (highest chart position: 20)

Warm Ways' b/w 'Blue Letter'
UK Single release: 7 November 1975 (did not chart)

'Rhiannon (Will You Ever Win)' b/w 'Sugar Daddy'
US single release: 4 February 1976 (highest chart position: 11).
Single mix available on 50 Years – Don't Stop.

'Over My Head' b/w 'I'm So Afraid'
UK single release: 27 February 1976 (did not chart)

'Rhiannon (Will You Ever Win)' b/w 'Sugar Daddy'
UK single release: 30 April 1976 (highest chart position: 46 on re-release in 1978)

'Say You Love Me' b/w 'Monday Morning'

US single release: 9 June 1976 (highest chart position: 11)
Single mix available on 25 Years – The Chain and 50 Years – Don't Stop.

'Say You Love Me' b/w 'Monday Morning'

UK single Release: 8 October 1976 (highest chart position: 40)

Why is this Fleetwood Mac album different from all other Fleetwood Mac albums? The answer is supergroup fragmentation in reverse: the addition of two singer-songwriters who, as Buckingham Nicks, were good enough – or so somebody thought – to do their own LP for Polydor a while back. And so, after five years of struggling for a consistency that became their hobgoblin, they make it sound easy. In fact, they come up with this year's easy listening classic. Roll on.

(Robert Christgau, *Village Voice*, 1975)

Fleetwood Mac, a deliberate, symbolic, prophetic album title, would be recorded in just ten days at Sound City in Van Nuys on the northern edge of Los Angeles.

Shortly before she and Buckingham joined Fleetwood Mac, Stevie Nicks picked up a novel called *Triad* at an airport. The book told the story of a Welsh woman who believes she's been possessed by another woman named Rhiannon. Nicks told Jim Ladd in 1976:

I wrote this song and made her into what I thought was an old Welsh witch. It's just about a very mystical woman that finds it very, very hard to be tied down in any kind of way. It wasn't until 1978 that I found out about *Mabinogion* (Welsh medieval prose tales) and that Branwen and Rhiannon are in there too, and that Rhiannon wasn't a witch at all; she was a mythological queen. But my story was definitely written about a celestial being. I didn't know who Rhiannon was exactly, but I knew she was not of this world.

'Rhainnon' is brilliantly produced: McVie, McVie, Fleetwood and Buckingham excel with their musical backing, Nicks' vocals are forceful and the glorious harmonies climb and fly above it all.

The first of Nicks' classic songs, 'Rhiannon' establishes her songwriting trope of verses and/or choruses built from repeating two or three simple chords: in this case Am to F in the verses, C to F in the chorus. This approach can be identified in 'Landslide' (C, G, Am), 'Dreams' (F and G), 'Gold Dust Woman' (D, G and C), 'Sisters Of The Moon' (Am to F), 'Sara' (F, G, Am) and others.

Keith Olsen: 'Stevie writes little repetitive loops that she crafts melodies around them. This is one of the unique aspects of the way she writes. Sometimes this gets old quickly, so a more commercial chordal form needs to be implemented. This is what she sometimes considers too much change from the original…'.

'I presented my songs to Lindsey on a cassette', Stevie said, 'which I would leave by the coffee pot, with a note saying, 'Here is a new song, You can produce it but don't change it'.

'My tendency is to want to add rhythm and to rock it up', Lindsay Buckingham recalled.

Buckingham's 'Monday Morning', upbeat and positive, was the ideal album opener. It was the most overtly commercial song so far recorded by Fleetwood Mac: a rocking 1975 update of the band's 1950s influences. The 2017 remastered version sounds utterly fabulous: the guitars shimmer, the bass grunts, the drums pound and the vocals soar.

The version of 'I'm So Afraid' here sounds very polite in comparison to the incendiary versions performed in concert in later years – the eight-minute version from *Fleetwood Mac Live,* recorded in Cleveland in 1980, is nothing short of explosive. Nevertheless, this studio version could sit happily on, say, *One of These Nights* or *Hotel California*. The seven-minute instrumental take on the deluxe edition of *Fleetwood Mac* is very good indeed.

'Landslide' was written in Aspen, Colorado: a song about the changes and challenges of life. Nicks composed the song while Lindsey Buckingham was on tour with Don Everly. Reflecting in 2014, she told the *New York Times*: 'I wrote 'Landslide' in 1973, when I was 27, and I did already feel old in a lot of ways. I'd been working as a waitress and a cleaning lady for years. I was tired'.

'Landslide' – with its close-mic'd vocals and delicate guitar solo – has become an AOR staple. A highlight of live performances since 1975, the song's reputation has grown throughout the years, with the Dixie Chicks taking it to a new audience with their country version: a number 7 hit in 2002.

'Landslide' and 'Rhiannon' both pre-date Buckingham and Nicks meeting Fleetwood and the McVies. These two songs – along with 'Monday Morning', 'I'm So Afraid' and 'I Don't Want To Know' – had been demoed by Buckingham and Nicks in 1974. 'Crystal' – a Nicks songs first released on *Buckingham Nicks* – was rearranged and re-recorded with reverential lead vocal from Lindsey Buckingham.

John McVie: 'I always thought 'Crystal' was the best song from Stevie and Lindsey. Wonderful music and lyrics. Gets me every time'.

Christine McVie hit a vein of mature, mid-paced love songs, composed on an electric piano in Malibu overlooking the Pacific: 'Say You Love Me', 'Over My Head', Warm Ways' and 'Sugar Daddy'.

'Say You Love Me' really swings, driven by rolling piano, the trademark off-kilter bass and drums, tambourine and, yes, banjo. It would be the band's preferred opening number in their live sets for years and would be the fourth single to be taken from the album (remixed with additional lead guitar) in June 1976.

'Over My Head' is an attractive ballad which, when released as a single, entered the US charts: Fleetwood Mac's first-ever hit there. The single remix is quite different, with more dobro and a far punchier production.

Christine McVie, interviewed by *Goldmine* in 1997:

('Over My Head') was the last track we worked on and we really didn't know what we were going to do with it. All it had was a vocal, a dobro guitar and a drum track – we weren't sure what to add to that. So I put on a little Vox Continental organ and Lindsey added some electric guitar, and it developed this really pleasant atmosphere. It didn't batter you. But it was the last track we ever thought would be a single.

'Warm Ways' has washes of wordless vocal harmonies, a confident lead vocal, and the classic mid-1970s instrumental line-of up acoustic rhythm guitar, electric lead guitar, electric piano, bass and drums.

'Sugar Daddy' is straight from the Stax/Atlantic soul songbook. Chris rocks out on the Hammond B3, Lindsey adds stinging guitar and the rhythm section pulsates, with a particularly brilliant bass part from John McVie.

Two further songs were recorded late in the sessions. 'World Turning' started as a studio jam. Its loose feeling was ideal for performing on stage and the song would become an in-concert monster, giving Mick Fleetwood his turn in the spotlight. Buckingham's lead guitar echoes Peter Green: even the song's title is borrowed from a Green song called 'The World Keeps On Turning', released on *Peter Green's Fleetwood Mac* in 1967.

"World Turning' allows Lindsey Buckingham to cut loose with some blues picking', says Mick Fleetwood, 'and he just kills it'.

'Blue Letter' is a rare cover version. This lively, radio-friendly number was a regular set-closer from 1975 to 1977. 'The idea (to record 'Blue Letter') came to us literally on the spot', wrote Fleetwood. 'The Curtis brothers (Michael and Richard) were recording demos at Sound City, and when we heard them play the song, we decided to give it a go.'

At the end of January, Buckingham and Nicks fulfilled their final obligations as a duo – concerts in Alabama, at the Morgan Auditorium of the University of Alabama in Tuscaloosa, and the Municipal Auditorium in Birmingham. The group had become an unlikely local sensation after progressive rock station WJLN-FM gave their album lots of airplay, particularly the spiralling 'Frozen Love'.

Playing for 7,000 people in Alabama 'really blew our minds', Buckingham said, 'going from being nobody in L.A. to being big stars in Birmingham – it was ridiculous'.

The Tuscaloosa shows were recorded to reel-to-reel by the in-house engineer. This remarkable recording shows Buckingham Nicks confidently performing most of their album, along with 'Blue Letter', 'I Don't Want To Know', 'Crystal', Monday Morning', 'Never Going Back Again' (instrumental at this stage), and the live debut of 'Rhiannon'.

In February 1975, Reprise released the only single from *Heroes Are Hard to Find*: Chris McVie's title track backed with Bob Welch's 'Born Enchanter'. It did not chart. Fleetwood Mac's next 'ten' singles would all make the top 20 in the US.

The album has been re-released twice. A 2004 single-disc version added the single remixes of 'Say You Love Me', 'Rhiannon', 'Over My Head' and 'Blue Letter'. A three-disc 'deluxe edition' from 2018 adds the four songs from the *Midnight Special* recording of January 1976, a funky if inconsequential one-chord jam called 'Jam #2', and early arrangements, takes or mixes of each song from the album, all of which sound curiously incomplete. None really add to the wider understanding of this landmark album. The full disc of live performances from October 1975 and February 1976 are revelatory, and proof – if it were needed – that Fleetwood Mac were always a killer live band.

On Tour, 1975
Live dates were booked whilst the album was still being recorded. A US tour from May to mid-June would be followed by another from late-July

through to the end of the year: almost one hundred shows in total in 1975, playing mid-sized arenas. Mick Fleetwood: 'It was a boot camp for Lindsey and Stevie who had to front the band, playing our new songs, some of their songs, as well as Bob's and Peter's'.

A typical setlist opened with three older songs: 'Get Like You Used to Be' from Christine McVie's Chicken Shack days, 'Station Man' from *Kiln House,* and 'Spare Me A Little Of Your Love' from *Bare Trees,* with added backing vocals. The bulk of the set would comprise nine of the eleven songs from *Fleetwood Mac*: 'Rhiannon', 'Monday Morning', 'Landslide', 'Crystal', 'Over My Head', 'Say You Love Me', 'I'm So Afraid', 'Blue Letter' and a set-closing 'World Turning'. 'Frozen Love' and 'Don't Let Me Down Again' from *Buckingham Nicks* would be given the Fleetwood Mac treatment. 'Why?' from *Mystery to Me* was given a scintillating three-part vocal harmony arrangement. In a nod to the band's past, Lindsey Buckingham dutifully sang 'Oh Well', 'The Green Manalishi (With The Two Prong Crown)', and the final encore: a seven-minute blissed-out 'Hypnotised'.

Rolling Stone in 2019:

('I'm So Afraid') immediately became a live showcase for Buckingham's guitar-playing. 'I'm no Jimi Hendrix,' he said when asked about his approach to guitar solos. 'I don't have the level of proficiency to just let myself go off into something completely different every night. Nor do I think I would want to. I am someone who values musical themes. Someone who feels there should be a consistency from night to night with something. I'm not one of those people that can slam out a completely different solo every night because I don't have the skill to do that.'

Back on tour after a six-week break, on 26 July, Fleetwood Mac supported ZZ Top at the City Park Stadium in New Orleans on a bill that also included Jeff Beck and Aerosmith. The following week, they performed the first of three consecutive summers at Bill Graham's season of shows at the Oakland Stadium, A Day On The Green. They were fourth on the bill with Robin Trower, Dave Mason, and headliner Peter Frampton, on the tour that gave the world *Frampton Comes Alive!* If tapes are to be believed, Fleetwood Mac opened their set with an instrumental version of Danny Kirwan's 'Sunny Side Of Heaven'.

Over the last weekend in August, three enormous concerts were held in California, at Anaheim Stadium (Saturday 30 August 1975), Balboa Stadium, San Diego (Sunday 31 August) and Madera Speedway, Fresno (Monday, 1 September). Fleetwood Mac supported Rod Stewart and the Faces at all of these, with two appearances each from Loggins and Messina, Lynyrd Skynyrd and Black Sabbath. On 21 September 1975, Fleetwood Mac performed at the Edgewater Raceway in Cincinnati, with the Eagles, The Marshall Tucker Band, Charlie Daniels and New Riders of The Purple Sage. At several dates in the northeast (Largo, Rochester, Uniondale, Philadelphia), they supported Loggins and Messina. This was a band that was paying its dues.

There are several live recordings from the tour. On 3 September 1975, Fleetwood Mac recorded a radio session at Trod Nossel Studios in Wallingford, Connecticut, performing their current set. Some sources date this to 23 September 1975, but the band were in La Crosse, Wisconsin, over 1000 miles to the west. Never available commercially, this was, for years, the only place to hear the band on their 1975 tour. By now a very tight band, they performed 'Get Like You Used To Be', 'Station Man', 'Spare Me A Little Of Your Love', 'Rhiannon', 'Why?', 'Landslide', 'Over My Head', 'I'm So Afraid', 'Oh Well', 'The Green Manalishi (With The Two Prong Crown)', 'World Turning', 'Blue Letter' and 'Hypnotised'.

Some of the shows in late October were also recorded and/or filmed.

5 October 1975 at Capital Centre, Largo, MD – an exhilarating hour-long set which is available on YouTube at the time of writing.

17 October 1975 at Capitol Theatre, Passaic, NJ – live versions of 'Get It Like You Used To Be', 'I'm So Afraid', 'Oh Well', The Green Manalishi (With The Two Prong Crown)', 'World Turning' and 'Blue Letter' were released on the 2018 expanded version of *Fleetwood Mac*. 'Don't Let Me Down Again' was included on *Fleetwood Mac Live* in 1980. Other songs from this show were broadcast on the King Biscuit Flower Hour and have been available on bootleg for years: 'Station Man', 'Spare Me A Little Of Your Love', 'Rhiannon', 'Landslide', 'I'm So Afraid', 'World Turning' and 'Hypnotised'.

25 October 1975 at the University of Connecticut, Storrs, CT – live versions of 'Station Man', 'Spare Me A Little Of Your Love', 'Rhiannon', 'Why?', 'Landslide', 'Don't Let Me Down Again' and 'Hypnotised' released on the 2018 expanded version of *Fleetwood Mac*.

Fleetwood Mac were once again a phenomenal live act, as these quite brilliant recordings attest.

'We spent the remainder of 1975 on a tour of colleges', Mick Fleetwood says, 'touring as we always had, in two station wagons with our gear in a trailer behind one of them. We drove ourselves. I couldn't have been happier – motion is my stasis and my comfort is what others consider chaos'.

'There were no limousines, and Christine slept on top of the amps in the back of the truck', Nicks recalls. 'We just played everywhere and we sold that record. We kicked that album in the ass.'

There's little doubt that their hard work as a touring band – over one hundred gigs in 1975, another forty in 1976 – combined with the clever musicianship of Buckingham and Nicks (and a hit single written by Christine McVie), significantly enhanced their popularity and subsequent album sales. That Buckingham and Nicks were both physically attractive, can't have hurt. Say what you like about Bob Welch's skills as a musician – and he had many – he wasn't exactly pin-up material. The success of 'Rhiannon' and the focus on Stevie Nicks, extended their reach as teenage girls started to buy Fleetwood Mac records for the first time.

Their tour ended at the two-day Diamond Head Festival in Honolulu, with sets from America, Bachman Turner Overdrive, Melissa Manchester, Herbie Hancock, Seals and Crofts, Tower of Power, Shawn Phillips, Cheech and Chong and others.

But the personal problems persisted. The McVies' marriage finally crumbled during this tour.

'I broke up with John in the middle of a tour', Christine recalled. 'I was aware of it being rather irresponsible. I had to do it for my sanity. It was either that or me ending up in a lunatic asylum.'

'You've got the pressure of being on the road and living with each other and seeing each other at their worst', John McVie reflected in 2003. 'Chris saw me at my worst one time too many. I drank too much, and when I've drunk too much, a personality comes out. It's not very pleasant to be around. And bless her heart, Chris said, 'I don't want to be around this person'. It was awful. You're told by someone you adore and love, and still do, that they don't want you in their life any more.'

'We literally didn't talk, other than to say, 'What key is this song in?', Christine recalled. 'We were as cold as ice to each other because John found it easier that way. Maybe we don't feel the same about each other anymore, but I wouldn't like to wipe that off the board.'

To make matters worse for McVie, his wife had taken up with the band's lighting director, Curry Grant, whose presence around the band caused friction. 'Wherever John was, he couldn't be', recalls Christine. 'There were some very delicate moments.'

'Over My Head'. Towards the end of 1975, something happened to the nation's AM radio playlists. It came on smoothly and softly, groping its way through the static on your tiny car speaker, fading in on a thick bed of electric organ and acoustic guitar, colored with lightly picked harmonics. You relaxed and let a few more miles drift by as sultry alto sang: 'You can take me to paradise/Then again you can be cold as ice/I'm over my head/ But it sure feels nice'. And it did feel nice.
(Samuel Graham, *Fleetwood Mac, the Authorised History,* 1978)

With help from a promotional boost by their record company – a $25,000 AM radio campaign – 'Over My Head' would become Fleetwood Mac's first-ever Top 20 hit in the US. 'Over My Head' was remixed for the single version: the fade-in intro that appeared on the album version was removed, new guitars were added in the chorus and different vocal harmonies were used. Many of the band's singles in the 1970s were given new mixes, including 'Say You Love Me', 'Rhiannon', 'Blue Letter', 'Think About Me', 'Sara', 'Sisters Of The Moon', and 'Not That Funny'.

1976

Enter Ken Caillat

With sessions for a new album due to begin at the end of January 1976, three other PR duties needed to be concluded: two mixing sessions and a TV show.

Firstly, the band entered Wally Heider Studios in Hollywood to mix the tapes of a live show recorded the previous October at the Capitol Theatre, Passaic, New Jersey. The mix engineer was Ken Caillat, who would be a key member of the Fleetwood Mac team for the next several years. While working on the song 'Rhiannon' for that radio show, Caillat said singer Stevie Nicks came up to him and asked if he could 'put a little fairy dust in my vocal'.

She must have liked what he did because he was soon hired to do the single mix of that same song. Ken Caillat:

On Monday, January 19, 1976, we were back in studio one and blew the doors off the mix for the radio edit of 'Rhiannon'. The fidelity of these studio tracks was far superior to that of the live radio show's tracks, so it really made my job a lot easier. I knew the song. I knew the structure, and, in this version, the instruments sounded huge. I knew this would be a great day. Keith Olsen had produced and mixed the album version of 'Rhiannon'. He had a particular talent for mixing, and one trick he liked to use was to emphasize the bottom end of the instruments. I, on the other hand, preferred to emphasize the midrange so that the instruments jumped out of the speakers more. I would compensate by increasing the volume of the bass instrument to support the extra mids and highs. Keith's tracks were a pleasure to work with. By the time the band arrived, the track already sounded pretty damn good. 'My God, man', Mick said when we walked in. 'That sounds amazing!'

Subsequently, Caillat was invited to join the band and co-producer Richard Dashut at The Record Plant studio in Sausalito for four months to record *Rumours*.

A few days later, Fleetwood Mac recorded a four-song set for *The Midnight Special* at the Burbank Studios. During Fleetwood Mac's second appearance on the show, they performed their latest single, 'Over My Head', a phenomenal version of 'Why?' from *Mystery to Me*, possibly the best ever version of 'Rhiannon' (Buckingham plays the Mick Taylor solo from the Rolling Stones' 'Bitch') and a tight take on 'World Turning'. *The Midnight Special* was broadcast on Thursday 8 April and no doubt helped push 'Rhiannon' to its peak of number 11 on the *Billboard* charts at the beginning of June. All four songs can be heard on the 2018 deluxe edition of *Fleetwood Mac*.

Rumours

Personnel:
Lindsey Buckingham: vocals, guitars, dobro, percussion, bass on 'Second Hand News'
Mick Fleetwood: drums, percussion, harpsichord
Stevie Nicks: vocals, tambourine
John McVie: bass guitar
Christine McVie: vocals, keyboards, synthesizer
Recorded February 1976–January 1977 at Criteria, Miami; Record Plant, Sausalito; Record Plant, Los Angeles; Zellerbach Auditorium, Berkeley; Wally Heider, San Francisco; Davlen, North Hollywood.
Produced by Ken Caillat, Richard Dashut and Fleetwood Mac.
Album release: February 1977. Highest chart placings: UK; 1 US: 1
Side one: 'Second Hand News', 'Dreams', 'Never Going Back Again', 'Don't Stop', 'Go Your Own Way', 'Songbird'
Side two: 'The Chain', 'You Make Loving Fun', 'I Don't Want To Know', 'Oh Daddy', 'Gold Dust Woman'

'Go Your Own Way' b/w 'Silver Springs'
US single release: 20 December 1976 (highest chart position: 10)
UK single release: 11 February 1977 (highest chart position: 38)
'Silver Springs' was first released on album in 1992 on *25 Years – The Chain*, and has since been made available on reissues of *Rumours*. A live version from May 1997 was released as a single and nominated for the Grammy Award for Best Pop Performance by a Duo or Group with Vocals in 1998.

'Dreams' b/w 'Songbird'
US release March/ April 1977 (highest chart position: 1). 'Dreams' re-entered the Billboard Hot 100 in October 2020 (highest position: 12).
UK single release: June 1977 (highest chart position: 24). 'Dreams' re-entered the UK charts in October 2020 (highest position: 35).

'Don't Stop' b/w 'Gold Dust Woman'
UK single release: 1 April 1977 (highest chart position: 32).

'Don't Stop' b/w 'Never Going Back Again'
US single release: July 1977 (highest chart position: 3)

'You Make Loving Fun' b/w 'Never Going Back Again'
UK single release: 30 September 1977 (highest chart position: 45)

'You Make Loving Fun' b/w 'Gold Dust Woman'
US single release 5 October 1977 (highest chart position: 9)

> A perfect album, made out of flaws in the human spirit.
> (Co-producer, Ken Caillat)

When Fleetwood Mac started recording *Rumours* at the Record Plant in Sausalito on 28 January 1976, they had yet to have a major hit single in the US. 'Over My Head' was working its way towards the *Billboard* top 20, and 'Rhiannon' and 'Say You Love Me' had not been released as singles. *Fleetwood Mac* would take several months to reach the top of the US charts, by when *Rumours* would be finished. So *Rumours* was not a follow-up to a successful album; it was simply the next Fleetwood Mac album.

That it was recorded at all was a triumph in itself.

Mick Fleetwood wrote in his memoirs:

> By the time we set about recording *Rumours,* we had fallen to pieces; after seven years, John and Christine called it quits, Lindsey and Stevie's four-year relationship was over, and my marriage to Jenny was on its way to divorce. We were all in an emotional ditch. Everybody knew everything about everyone. But I was definitely piggie-in-the-middle, though in actual fact, my marriage was going down the tubes too. But I was spared the in-house up-front situation. I didn't have to actually work with my ex-spouse! As 'Rhiannon' began to climb the charts and our debut album reaches sales of a million copies, I knew there was only one way for this to work. We had to get out of L.A. and live together, the way we had when we were at Kiln House, because once again, we were in critical condition.

Fleetwood rented a house in Florida.

From *Rolling Stone* in 2019:

> In 1976, early in the recording process of what would come to be Fleetwood
> Mac's epochal album *Rumours,* they took some time off from touring and
> rented a house to work on new material. With the two relationships at
> the centre of the band unravelling, it may not have been the best time for
> a family vacation: 'Aside from the obvious unstated tension, I remember
> the house having a distinctly bad vibe to it, as if it was haunted, which did
> nothing to help matters,' Mick Fleetwood wrote in his memoirs.

Fleetwood remarked later:

> The divorce didn't really hit me too hard at first because I just kept
> working on the band. The McVies' marriage cracked up for good, while we
> were living in a rented house in Florida, having taken some time off from
> touring. We decided to use the vacation to rehearse and write for the next
> album. That was our attitude; no matter how awful things became, the
> band had to come first. John and I became very close to each other again
> because our marriages were both failing. We rode around the USA in our
> station wagons and talked and talked. That's how we got through.

Stevie Nicks, Buckingham and Christine McVie had been writing new
songs: songs about each other, their relationships and feelings. '*Rumours*
sold a storyline', writes Rob Trucks. 'No review, interview or feature about
the band was written without assessing the recent break-up of Christine
McVie from John McVie, of Stevie Nicks from Lindsey Buckingham. And
how the songs of *Rumours* sprang from these separations.'

Buckingham's brittle 'Second Hand News' ('One thing I think you
should know/I ain't gonna miss you when you go') is reflected in Nicks'
gentle, mesmerizing 'Dreams' ('Now here you go again/You say you
want your freedom'). Buckingham ups the ante with 'Never Going Back
Again' ('Been down one time/Been down two times/I'm never going back
again'), and pushes more forcefully in 'Go Your Own Way': a harsh kiss-off
('Loving you isn't the right thing to do/Packing up/Shacking up is all you
want to do'). Nicks in 1977:

> On this album, all the songs that I wrote except maybe 'Gold Dust
> Woman' – and even that comes into it – are definitely about the people in
> the band… Chris' relationships, John's relationship, Mick's relationship,

Lindsey's and mine. They're all there and they're very honest, and people will know exactly what I'm talking about… people will really enjoy listening to what happened since the last album.

Meanwhile, Christine's songs either celebrate new love or, as in one case, communicate a warm-hearted but still painful message to her ex-husband.

'I'd be sitting there in the studio while they were mixing 'Don't Stop'', John said later, 'and I'd listen to the words which were mostly about me, and I'd get a lump in my throat. I'd turn around and the writer's sitting right there'.

'You Make Loving Fun' was written by McVie's estranged wife for the new man in her life, Curry Grant.

'I thought (at first) I was drying up', Christine McVie told *Q* magazine years later. 'I was practically panicking because every time I sat down at a piano, nothing came out. Then, one day I just sat down and wrote the four and a half songs of mine (that are) on the album.'

Buckingham told *Uncut* in 2003:

You can look at *Rumours* and say, 'Well, the album is bright and it's clean and it's sunny'. But everything underneath is so dark and murky. What was going on between us created a resonance that goes beyond the music itself. You had these dialogues shooting back and forth about what was going down between us and we were chronicling every nuance of it. We had to play the hand out and people found it riveting. It wasn't a press creation. It was all true and we couldn't suppress it. The built-in drama cannot be underplayed as a springboard to that album's success.

The following month they moved back to California to start recording. 'I'd heard great things about the Record Plant in Sausalito, across the bay from San Francisco', Fleetwood wrote. 'It came with a house overlooking the water, that we could live in while recording. I booked it for two months and in February we made the move up there.'

'That house was like the riot house', Nicks told *Uncut* in 2003. 'There were girls everywhere and everybody was completely drunk the whole time. Me and Chris decided we couldn't be there. The next day, we moved out and got two matching apartments next to each other.'

In Frank Moriarty's book, *Seventies Rock: The Decade of Creative Chaos*, Stevie Nicks is quoted from a *Creem* interview in July 1977, explaining tension during the sessions: 'We were all trying to break up, and when you break up with someone, you don't want to see him. You especially don't want to eat breakfast with him the next morning, see him all day and all night, and all day the day after … '.

Christine said:

Trauma. Trau-ma. The sessions were like a cocktail party every night – people everywhere. We ended up staying in these weird hospital rooms … and of course, John and me were not exactly the best of friends. We had two alternatives – go our own ways and see the band collapse, or grit our teeth and carry on playing with each other. Normally when couples split, they don't have to see each other again. We were forced to get over these differences.

Describing the mood of the sessions, *Rumours* co-producer Richard Dashut, said: 'Defences were wearing thin and they were quick to open up their feelings. Instead of going to friends to talk it out, their feelings were vented through their music: the album was about the only thing they had left'.

Amongst all of this, Christine started a relationship with the band's lighting director Curry Grant. She has said that she wrote 'Oh Daddy' for Mick Fleetwood: then separated from Jenny Boyd, the mother of his two children. It seems just as likely that the song is about Curry Grant.

Oh Daddy
You soothe me with your smile
You're letting me know
You're the best thing in my life

'During *Rumours*', Ken Caillat remembers, 'there was a lot of tension on the romantic side from every band member, Richard and I considered wearing helmets, these were real-life romances ending, with real tears and real emotion … and I believe that *Rumours* would not sound like it does if things had been different'.

'Everybody was pretty weirded-out', Christine McVie explained. 'Somehow Mick was there, the figurehead: "We must carry on … let's be mature about this, sort it out". Somehow we waded through it.'

'Keep Me There'
The first song laid down was Christine McVie's 'Keep Me There' – demoed as 'Butter Cookie'.

Wrote Ken Caillat:

'Keep Me There' was a fairly typical Christine McVie song, with verse, chorus, verse, chorus, instrumental break, chorus. Except, as the band played it down, a musical tension developed that needed to be released from the song. So, after the last chorus, they started playing a jam or tag out, where everyone played hot and heavy. John started it with an amazing bass line in the break before the tag.

John McVie:

That was an Olympic fretless bass. And I was messin' about in the studio and I just played the riff. Chris said 'Oh! I like that!'. So we kept it in. If I had my way, I would've brought the band in a little earlier on the ending... it tends to stand out and look a little lonely out there, but it seems to work.

Ken Caillat:

Christine and Lindsey started playing off each other for about three minutes. Each time they played the song, it got better. Something amazing was taking shape. It was a potential hit song. The band members took off their headphones and piled into the control room, finding places to sit so they could listen to what they'd just laid down. Lindsey was visibly excited, rubbing his hands together. Christine was giggling with excitement.

For now, the song was left as it was – to be worked on further, later in the sessions. Another version was recorded on 25 February. Both the 'Butter Cookie' demo and two takes of 'Keep Me There' can be heard on the 35th anniversary release of *Rumours*.

'Go Your Own Way'
Lindsay Buckingham had been tinkering with 'Go Your Own Way' since the previous summer.

'It may have been the first song that I played as an offering to the band', he says. 'It was in Miami. I played it for them, and it met with such a strong response. It really broke the ice and set the tone for the album in general. It got everyone off on the right foot and let everyone feel that we had a strong place to go.'

'Go Your Own Way' started as a basic cassette demo, with just a loudly-strummed acoustic and intense vocal.

'Lindsey was beating his acoustic guitar as hard as he could and screaming his lungs out', Ken Caillat recalled.

The basic take was recorded by all five members of the band together, with Buckingham playing his 1959 Fender Stratocaster. It is perhaps Mick Fleetwood's drum patterns that are the key 'hook' in this song. The switch to straight 4/4 time in the chorus provides an amazing rush of adrenalin. 'Lindsey had this very specific idea for the drum parts he wanted', Fleetwood remarks. 'But one thing he didn't realize was that I couldn't play them. And it blew his mind!'

Ken Caillat recalls.

The right drum approach was crucial. One day, Lindsey came in and said he'd heard 'Street Fighting Man' by The Rolling Stones, and he thought that kind of feel would work well. I remember watching him guide Mick as to what he wanted – he'd be so animated, like a little kid, playing these air tom fills with his curly hair flying. Mick wasn't so sure he could do what Lindsey wanted, but he did a great job, and the song took off.

Mick Fleetwood:

The rhythm was a tom-tom structure that Lindsey demoed by hitting Kleenex boxes or something. I never quite got to grips with what he wanted, so the end result was my mutated interpretation. It became a major part of the song, a completely back-to-front approach that came, I'm ashamed to say, from capitalising on my own ineptness. There was some conflict about the 'crackin' up, shackin' up' line, which Stevie felt was unfair, but Lindsey felt strongly about. It was basically, 'On your bike, girl!'.

'I very, very much resented him telling the world that 'packing up, shacking up' with different men was all I wanted to do', Stevie Nicks told *Rolling Stone* in 1997. 'He knew it wasn't true. It was just an angry thing that he said. Every time those words would come out onstage, I wanted to go over and kill him. He knew it, so he really pushed my buttons through that.'

'Go Your Own Way' was ultimately edited from two takes – the edit is at around 2:50. Ken Caillat wrote later:

I played take fourteen and found a likely spot to make the edit. Then I cut off the front half of fourteen and put it on the table, still on the front reel. I got out another take-up reel, found the same spot in take 25, and made the cut again, then I grabbed the first reel from the table, took a breath, and placed the good front half on the left reel holder and the good back half on the right reel holder. I took the two ends that I had cut and laid them down on the two-inch splicing block, making sure they touched perfectly, then I cut off a piece of splicing tape and stuck it across the spot where both ends touched and rubbed the tapes firmly down. Now I had one song again, spliced from two takes.

'Gold Dust Woman'

Next, the band started work on Stevie Nicks' classic 'Gold Dust Woman', a song that still has the power to startle after forty-five years and 20 million record sales.

Rolling Stone discussed it in 2019:

The chilling climax of *Rumours* is a seductive guitar ballad that doubles as a horror show. Nicks sings about a dark, sexual obsession and a drug rush as if they're the same addiction, taunting, 'Did she make you cry?/Make you break down?/Shatter your illusions of love?', over woozy, phased guitars. Nicks still performs 'Gold Dust Woman' live, with an interpretive dance. 'It's me being some of the drug addicts I knew, and probably being myself too – just being that girl lost on the streets, freaked-out with no idea how to find her way,' she told Rolling Stone. 'When Christine saw it, she said, 'Wow, we've always known that "Gold Dust Woman" was about the serious drug days, but this really depicts how frightening it was for all of us and what we were willing to do for it.' We were dancing on the edge for years.'

Nicks says:

'Gold Dust Woman' was a little bit about drugs. At that time, everybody around me was doing (them)', 'Lindsey and I wonder, if we hadn't moved to L.A., would we ever have got into drugs? Drug-taking was methodical when we got to L.A.. It was, 'Here, try this'. Everybody was so willing to give you stuff and tell you you'd like it. 'Gold Dust Woman' was about how we all love the ritual of it, the little bottle, the diamond-studded spoons, the fabulous velvet bags. For me, it fitted right into the incense and candles and (all) that stuff. And I really imagined that it could overtake everything, never thinking in a million years that it would overtake me.

'Oh Daddy'

Mick Fleetwood: "Oh, Daddy' is a lesson in less-is-more. It's one of my favourite songs that Christine has ever recorded. I think it's a fantastic song'.

Stevie Nicks: 'That's probably my favourite Christine song of all time and probably one of the only dark songs she wrote'.

This simply beautiful, spacious, opaque song is one of those half-forgotten gems in the Fleetwood Mac back catalogue – if a song on one of the best-selling albums of all-time can ever be half-forgotten.

Ken Caillat recalls:

Everything with this song depended on Christine's organ part. It carried the entire track. Christine played her organ with her spinning Leslie speaker set on slow rotate, turning only a few times a minute. I had mic'd the speakers so that the organ moved eerily between each of my big control room speakers. John's moving bass line supported the whole sonic structure, like the foundation of a house. Finally, Lindsey's electric guitar, his Fender Strat – set in reverb and multiple delays – penetrated the sonic soup much as low-beam headlights cut through fog. On the last take, very near the end, Christine thought that she had made a mistake, and she tried to get our attention by hitting some odd notes on the organ at 3:42 into the song, trying to stop everyone from playing so that we would do another take. But nobody noticed. We finished that take, and it had the magic we were looking for. We ended up leaving those Bep! Bep! Bep! moments in the final version of the song on the album. They were random at the time, but they really worked for us, even through the final edit. They just added something that we all loved.

Lindsey Buckingham, on *Classic Albums*:

It's funny how certain little things happen by accident in any creative process and get left in, because somehow they are happy accidents. You kind of have to be on the lookout for those things. Sometimes something very small can create an ambiance and magic and something that would be less if it didn't exist. There is a keyboard blip on the end, which was not something she was playing interpretively. You know… it wasn't jazz! It was just her saying, hey what are you doing in there? And it got left in there… just one of things you wait for.

'Second Hand News'

On a roll, Fleetwood Mac started their fifth song of the sessions. This song had the working title, 'Strummer', but eventually became the album's upbeat opening song, 'Second Hand News'.

'For his next song, Lindsey gave us only his chord ideas', says Ken Caillat. '(He) didn't have any lyrics for us to hear. At the time, I didn't understand why Lindsey kept his lyrics from us. Later, I learned it was because he knew that Stevie would get into an argument with him when she heard them, and he didn't want to have another fight with her over his song lyrics.'

I know there's nothing to say
Someone has taken my place
When times go bad, when times go rough
I'm just second hand news

Buckingham, interviewed on *Classic Albums*:

I think we had a working title of 'Strummer' because it did start off as a kind of a strummy, acoustic feel. But I think the intent for that song was to be kind of a dance beat. I know Richard Dashut and I had been driving around from town to town during those days and had heard 'Jive Talkin'' by the Bee Gees. And we really liked the feel of that, and they had a rolling kind of thing behind it. That was always my intention for the feel that it should have. And I think eventually we got there.

'Second Hand News' originally featured a flowing and melodic John McVie bass part. This can be heard on the original take released on the 35th-anniversary edition of *Rumours*, along with a much sparser early version. Lindsey Buckingham replaced the bass part later on in the sessions.

'You Make Loving Fun'
Christine McVie

'You Make Loving Fun' was pretty basic, and Lindsey wasn't there when we started to record it. So, I had the luxury of building the song on my own.

'You Make Loving Fun' started as a riff, as Ken Caillat recalls:

Since we'd arrived at the Record Plant, Christine had been playing this one riff, off and on. That day Christine said she wanted to cut a new song, and I found out that her idling riff actually had a name. 'It's called "You Make Loving Fun"', she said. 'Sounds great, Chris!', I said. 'Why don't we start working it out while we wait for everyone else to arrive?' Christine sat down at the Rhodes and played the keys hard, almost making the sound growl. The action on a Rhodes – being a mellow and cooler-sounding instrument – is such that you have to really attack it to get it to growl. We wanted to make it even crunchier, so we ran it through an amp, cranking it up. Mick and John arrived.

They set up a clavinet – an electrically amplified clavichord – through a wah-wah pedal for added colour. 'After a couple of takes', Caillat recalled, 'we realized that Christine couldn't play the clav part and the wah-wah rhythm at the same time'. Mick Fleetwood operated the pedal for the final take. Hammond organ can also be heard at the back of the mix.

With work on 'You Make Loving Fun' completed, after just one week of sessions, Fleetwood Mac had recorded six new songs.

'Songbird'
Christine McVie:

'Songbird' was written in about half an hour. Stevie and I were in a condominium block, and the boys were all in the Sausalito Record Plant house raving with girls and boozing and everything. I had a little transistorised electric piano next to my bed, and I woke up one night at about 3:30 a.m. and started playing it. I had it all, words, melody, chords in about 30 minutes. It was like a gift from the angels, but I had no way to record it. I thought I'm never gonna remember this. So I went back to bed, and couldn't sleep. Next day, I went into the studio shaking like a leaf 'cause I knew it was something special. That's how I like to write songs. I wrote the chords and the words and the melody almost as if it was coming from someone else and not me. If I could write a few more like that, I would be a happy girl.

Although Christine has never said as much explicitly ('It doesn't really relate to anybody in particular; it relates to everybody. A lot of people play it at their weddings or at bar mitzvahs, or at their dog's funeral. It's universal. It's about you and nobody else. It's about you and everybody else'), there's little doubt that her relationship with Curry Grant is the subject of one of her greatest songs.

The first version of 'Songbird' recorded at the Record Plant in mid-February 1976 – as heard on the expanded reissue of *Rumours* – sounds tentative and hesitant: as though Christine McVie is holding back. At the suggestion of engineer and co-producer, Ken Caillat, the final take of the last track on side one of *Rumours* would be recorded away from the Record Plant.

Caillat wrote:

A few months before working with Fleetwood, I had been the main engineer on Joni Mitchell's tour and I had recorded twelve of her live concerts. 'Songbird' felt to me like it should have a live sound; the depth of a concert hall. I tried adding some reverb to Christine's piano and vocal, but it sounded corny. One of the Joni Mitchell shows I recorded had been in the Berkeley Community Theater, near the Record Plant. I showed the band what 'Songbird' could sound like with live-sounding reverb. Then I had a brilliant idea. 'Hey, let's record it live over at the Berkeley Community Theater! It's a beautiful-sounding hall. I recently recorded Joni there.' Mick, Christine and Lindsey gave me their nod of approval. 'Great, I'll start to make arrangements tomorrow.'

The Berkeley Community Theater was unavailable, but Caillat was able to book the nearby Zellerbach Hall Auditorium on the campus of the University of California for 6 March, three weeks ahead.

Ken Caillat placed flowers on a nine-foot grand piano and requested three spotlights to illuminate the flowers from above. Four microphones were placed around the piano and another eight around the auditorium. To maintain tempo, and to allow Christine McVie to focus on performing, Lindsey Buckingham strummed an acoustic guitar to a click track. This guitar track was fed to McVie's headphones. In the end, she recorded the piano first and added the vocals later. Ken Caillat:

Christine is a natural performer, and this was a challenge for her. I felt bad for her, but it was the only way we could get the clarity and flexibility we wanted for the recording. By this time, it was already after midnight, and she was starting to get tired and cranky. It didn't help that we had to keep stopping because Lindsey would forget and play too loud. We'd hear his guitar in the ambience mics again, and we'd have to stop the take. We asked for everyone's patience, and about 1 a.m., we got the perfect piano take. After singing all night in her head, Christine could finally stand onstage and sing the song aloud. She sang to the final piano take, playing in her headphones. I expected her voice to reverberate throughout the hall, creating the perfect natural reverb, but it didn't. She was singing up close and personal to our expensive microphone, so we got only minimal reverberation. 'Okay', I said. 'Let's just get the vocal and worry about the reverb later.' 'Thank you, Ken. I want to go home', she said. She got the perfect vocal in less than an hour.

For extra depth and reverberation, Caillat fed the vocal track through the hall's stage speakers out into the hall and recorded it once again.

John McVie: ''Songbird' used to get to me. I don't think it was anything to do with what happened with Chris and me. It was more the total aura of the song'.

'Silver Springs'

Ken Caillat: 'Stevie had a cassette of a song called 'Silver Springs', that she'd written while she and Lindsey were on the road in Maryland: she'd seen the sign 'Silver Spring, Maryland', and she liked the name. She wanted the song to be her epic moment on *Rumours*'.

The district of Silver Spring (note, no 's') is on the northern edge of Washington, D.C.. The band will have passed through, travelling from Richmond to Largo along Highway 495 on 5 October 1975.

'I got the idea from a freeway sign as we drove under the sign that said Silver Springs, Maryland', Nicks said. 'And… that's the kind of writer that I am. If I hear a name I really like, I can maybe write a story about it. Silver Springs sounded like a pretty fabulous place to me. And, 'You could be my silver springs…', that's just a whole symbolic thing of what you (meaning Lindsay Buckingham) could have been to me.'

The song was Nicks' condemnation of Buckingham: of his inability to let her love him.

Time casts a spell on you, but you won't forget me
And I know I could have loved you, but you would not let me
I'll follow you down 'til the sound of my voice will haunt you

'Silver Springs' was initially recorded with electric guitar, drums and bass, with Nicks on Fender Rhodes piano and guide vocal. It was later re-cut on 14 February 1976 by all five musicians in the studio together, with take eight as the master. 'Gold Dust Woman' was re-recorded on the same day, with take four marked as 'best'. Both would have many subsequent overdubs.

'Dreams'
'Stevie one day (in late February) wrote this song down the hall at the Record Plant', recalls Ken Caillat. 'She came bursting through the doors of the control room and said, 'You guys won't believe what I just wrote: I wrote 'Dreams', it's amazing'.'

Nicks said, on *Classic Albums*:

'Dreams' was written on one of those nights where there was nothing for me to do. So I went down the hall (to) a black and red room with a sunken pit in the middle where there was a piano, and Sly Stone's big, black-velvet bed. I sat down on the bed with my keyboard in front of me… and wrote 'Dreams' in about ten minutes. I knew it was something special and I was not self-conscious or insecure about showing it to the rest of the band.

'We said, let's hear it', Caillat remembers. 'She starts playing her three chords. Lindsey starts playing his guitar. Mick starts playing whatever he can beat on. John starts playing his bass. This song is just 10 minutes old.'

Christine McVie, interviewed in 1992 when promoting *The Chain*:

When Stevie first played it for me on the piano, it was just three chords and one note in the left hand. I thought, 'This is really boring'. But the Lindsey genius came into play and he fashioned three sections out of identical chords, making each section sound completely different. He created the impression that there's a thread running through the whole thing.

'Dreams' was an interesting outcome for something which didn't have a lot of variety in terms of its chord structures but had tons of variety in terms of its melodic left and right turns. There is no drama without contrast.

The lyrics of 'Dreams' directly reflecting Nicks' painful breakup with Buckingham:

But listen carefully to the sound
Of your loneliness
Like a heartbeat… drives you mad
In the stillness of remembering what you had

It was recorded with drums, bass, organ, acoustic guitar, Rhodes piano and lead vocals. An early take can be heard on the 2004 and 2012 reissues of *Rumours*.

Towards the end of the sessions at the Record Plant, looking for ideas to improve the song, Lindsey Buckingham suggested reworking 'Dreams' with a more hypnotic drum part, with the idea of snipping and looping eight bars of perfect drumming. Such is Fleetwood's idiosyncratic style that they were unable to find what they needed in any of the existing takes of 'Dreams'.

'We made a (new) eight-bar loop of Mick's playing', says Ken Caillat, 'which created this fantastic, deep hypnotic effect. It's funny, but when people talk about the classic rhythm section of Mick Fleetwood and John McVie and they point to this one song, I'm always amused that they're talking about a drum loop'.

Stevie Nicks added her lead vocal but couldn't match the mood of the original.

Ken Caillat:

The first time she sang ('Dreams'), she did such a great job. Typically we call that a work vocal, just a guide track that we plan on replacing later. But we tried to replace that lead vocal throughout the rest of the year, and there was some parts of the verses we could never beat. She could never improve the vocal part, so there was some sort of spontaneity that came with her first performance of that.

At these same sessions, John McVie added his distinctive bass guitar ('Make it as simple as possible… give it a lot of air and space. It allows the rest of the song to have sort of an ethereal quality'), Christine McVie contributed Hammond organ, and Lindsey Buckingham provided electric and acoustic guitars. Months later, piano, backing vocals and percussion completed this masterful track.

In autumn 1977, 'Dreams' would become Fleetwood Mac's only number one single in America.

'Think About It'

A Nicks/Buckingham duet, written by Nicks with Bruce Springsteen's pianist, Roy Bittan. It has a country twang and uses a straightforward rock track: drums, bass, electric guitar, organ and vocals. Recorded quickly in eight takes, it was later overdubbed with guitars, bass and background vocals.

'About halfway through the *Rumours* recording, we stopped working on Stevie's song 'Think About It'', Ken Cailatt said. 'She had too many songs.'

Nicks re-recorded 'Think About It' for her solo album, *Bella Donna*, in 1981. Fleetwood Mac's version finally saw release in 2004 on the expanded reissue of *Rumours*.

'Don't Stop'

Originally titled 'Yesterday's Gone', this Christine McVie song has joint lead vocals with Lindsey Buckingham.

'We shared verses', says Buckingham, 'and mine was first. It kind of muddied the lines of whose song it was. But it really was kind of a great collaboration in the sense that some of hers and mine musical senses overlap… and I think it worked very well to the advantage of that song'.

Buckingham: 'Don't stop'
McVie: 'Thinking about tomorrow'
Buckingham: 'Don't stop'
McVie: 'It'll soon be here'
Buckingham: 'It'll be'
McVie: 'Better than before'
Both: 'Yesterday's gone, yesterday's gone'

It's a song of optimistic advice to ex-husband John McVie – 'I love you, but I'm not in love with you'. As Christine put it, ''Don't Stop' was just a feeling. It seemed like a pleasant revelation to have. It would make a great song for an insurance company, but I'm definitely not a pessimist. I'm basically a love-song writer'.

''Don't Stop' was always tough for me because it is a shuffle', co-producer Ken Caillat recalls. 'I couldn't get enough definition on the instruments. It was like everybody was playing all at once'.

The basic track combined drums, bass, electric guitar and electric piano with Christine's live guide vocals. She and Lindsey would later re-sing the song as a duet, and the electric piano was replaced with an upright tack piano during August sessions at Wally Heider's in Hollywood.

'I worked my butt off to get the bass and kick (drum) up', Caillat said. 'It came out okay. The vocals were great with Lindsey and Chris' duet and the choir at the end. We wanted a lot of voices to sing the ending, so we got everyone who worked at the Record Plant to come into the big room and sing. There were dogs, kids and a lot of fun!'

'Never Going Back Again', 'Doesn't Anything Last', 'Planets Of The Universe' and 'Smile At You'
Lindsey Buckingham, interviewed on *Classic Albums*:

I remember writing ('Never Going Back Again') when we got off the road. It was written about a girl that I had met in New England and spent a very short amount of time with. Someone who really, initially, didn't want to spend time with me, and I talked her into it. And of course, 'Been down one time, Been down two times, Never going back again', is really a sweet sentiment. It's a naïve sentiment. Because every time you are happy, you create this illusion for yourself that you're never gonna be unhappy again. Life doesn't really work that way, and you have to learn to accept that you'll have ups and downs your entire life. So that was really the sentiment of the song for me.

'Never Going Back Again' went through several iterations over the course of the recording sessions. At its heart, a finger-picked acoustic folk song, it was not recorded seriously at this first set of sessions. The music, at least, dates back several years – it was performed at the Buckingham Nicks concerts in 1975, introduced as 'a little guitar thing'.

'We weren't clear initially on how we wanted to approach it', Buckingham says. 'I think Mick had put some brushes on it and therefore, we had the working title of 'Brushes'.'

A piece called 'Brushes' can be heard on the expanded *Rumours* sets – this does not have any vocals, nor, ironically, any of Mick Fleetwood's brushwork. Another instrumental, with brushes this time, is on the 2012 set, and a faster take played on either dobro or electric guitar is on both. There is also a vocal duet with Nicks with acoustic guitar, percussion and a guitar solo on the 2012 release.

'Eventually, it got paired down to just two guitars', Buckingham notes. 'A left and right guitar. It did go through its own evolution of trying other things. I think the initial attempt was going to be a more orchestral approach, a more layered approach. But I think eventually we came back to a simple approach which was suited to the sentiment of the song.'

'Doesn't Anything Last' is a strong, slow but unfinished Buckingham song. There is a 70-second demo on the expanded *Rumours* sets and a very country-flavoured (and very short) Buckingham/Nicks duet on the 2012 box set.

'Planets Of The Universe' is presented as a basic vocals/guitar/bass/demo on the reissued *Rumours*. It's a curio here, despite strong vocals from Nicks. It was eventually recorded for *Trouble in Shangri-La*: Nicks' sixth album, released in 2001. One of the original verses, beginning, 'You will remember, but I will die a slow death', was removed. Another new Stevie Nicks song called 'Smile At You' was started but remained unfinished. It would be attempted again for *Tusk* before finally being recorded for *Say You Will* in 2001-2002.

After nine weeks at the Record Plant, Fleetwood Mac concluded their sessions there on 10 April 1976. They had completed basic recordings of nine of the eleven songs ultimately released on the album, plus the B-side, 'Silver Springs'. But the album was far from finished.

Back on the Road

Fleetwood Mac returned to live concerts for a handful of dates in April and May, supported by Gary Wright, Status Quo and/or UFO. The 1976 setlist dropped 'The Green Manalishi', 'Station Man', 'Frozen Love' and 'Get Like You Used To Be', adding 'Go Your Own Way', 'You Make Loving Fun', 'Dreams' and 'Silver Springs'. They also appeared again as part of the 'Day on the Green' concerts, supporting Peter Frampton at Oakland Coliseum in front of 75,000 fans.

Stevie Nicks, interviewed by Andy Capper in 2005:

The most memorable day I ever had was when I was 29. We played the 'Day on the Green' concert in San Francisco. The concert was a tribute to the success of *Frampton Comes Alive!*. And we played before Peter.

One of these concerts was recorded and filmed – the live version of 'Over My Head' from 2 May 1976 at the Campus Field, University

of California, Santa Barbara, was included on the deluxe reissue of
Fleetwood Mac. Parts of this show were included in a 30-minute
promotional film called *Rosebud*, released the following year. Ken Caillat:

> When I watch it now, I can see that 'Go Your Own Way' didn't have the
> end solo that it has on the album, because it hadn't been invented yet.
> The same was true of the other new songs they played that day. We still
> had months to go in the recording process, but all-in-all, it was a great
> day. The band seemed as if they had healed from their recent breakups.

A week later, Fleetwood Mac were filmed performing a concert-length
show for family and friends at Studio Instrument Rentals in Los Angeles.
Parts of this were used in the *Rosebud* promo film.

Wally Heider's Studio 4

Fleetwood Mac continued work on *Rumours* at Wally Heider's Studio
Four in Hollywood, starting on 14 May and running to early June. Stevie
Nicks and Christine McVie were on holiday, so sessions concentrated
on a series of Lindsey Buckingham overdubs on existing songs and the
recording of a new one. Firstly, Buckingham added a new, simpler bass
part to 'Second Hand News'. Ken Caillat:

> The bass made a huge difference. John's old version was a brilliant
> walking bass line, which meant that it moved more and played more
> notes than Lindsey's. Lindsey's was very simple and sparse, playing only
> a single bass note in each bar of the chorus. 'Lindsey, are you going to
> have John replay your bass part when he returns?', I asked, knowing how
> sensitive John was about his bass-playing and, especially, about criticism
> from the young Lindsey. The fact that Lindsey had not only criticized it
> but had also replaced it with a much more simple, straightforward part,
> meant that this would be a touchy subject. 'Uh, yeah. That should be
> interesting', Lindsey said, laughing nervously.

New drum parts were added to 'Second Hand News'.
Ken Caillat wrote:

> Mick was very unsure of what Lindsey wanted, and his first attempt was
> horrible. Mick was a very elegant drummer, and his fills were nothing less
> than genius. But that was not what Lindsey was going for. Mick tried five

or six times. Then he finally said, 'Why don't you have a go at it, Linds? Then maybe I'll get the idea'. I rewound the tape and played the section again. This time Lindsey played the part, and he was wildly animated, his arms flailing in the air, holding Mick's drumsticks. He wasn't elegant at all, but he played like a man driven from deep inside. After Lindsey finished showing Mick what he wanted, Mick said, 'I'm sorry, Lindsey, but I just don't think I can play it the way you want. I like what you played. Let's just use your version'. Lindsey was, I believe, relieved at this outcome. It was out in the open now, and Lindsey was free to play other people's parts. We ran the song down three or four more times, and Lindsey played the tom parts throughout the song. Lindsey had a brilliance, and he was crucial to the band's success. The biggest problem with Lindsey though, was that he couldn't communicate his ideas without coming off as uptight. This tended to make everyone else in the band feel defensive. Sometimes it felt as if you could cut the tension with a knife. Lindsey just couldn't cross that bridge to constructive criticism. You can hear Lindsey's wild tom part played at 0:38, 1:28, 1:44, 1:53, and 2:00 on 'Second Hand News'.

This was embellished by a percussive effect created by hitting the seat of a chair. 'Lindsey was the accent king', Caillat marvelled. 'He could accent with guitars, he could accent with toms, he could accent with Naugahyde chairs.'

Lindsey Buckingham pointed out that 'Found sounds have always been something that interested me.' Buckingham also replaced his lead vocal, part of which wordlessly doubled the short guitar solo.

'Gold Dust Woman' was given a dobro overdub: two separate parts were recorded and it can be heard throughout the song, but listen for picking at 4:07 and accenting chords at 4:14 and 4:18.

'Never Going Back Again' was re-recorded. The result: two minutes of genius. 'I wanted to get the best sound on every one of his picking parts', Caillat said. He asked Buckingham to re-string his guitar every twenty minutes:

I'm sure the roadies wanted to kill me. Re-stringing the guitar three times every hour was a bitch. But Lindsey had lots of parts on the song, and each one sounded magnificent. The only problem was, when Lindsey went to sing, he realized that he played all of his guitar parts in the wrong key. Oh, man! So we recorded everything all over again the next day, dispensing with the changing of guitar strings – we had to lose all of that so we could get Lindsey singing in the right key.

'Silver Springs' was given a new guitar part. Ken Caillat:

> I had eight inputs from Lindsey's one guitar part: the tiny noise of his
> plastic guitar pick or his fingernails striking the strings, the dry direct
> guitar sound coming through my Fat Box, two mics on his electric guitar
> amplifier, two more mics on the rotating Leslie, and the reverb return from
> the delay machine rejoining all of the sounds about a quarter second late.
> I could put all of these sounds together in any combination, using the left,
> right, and centre panning positions. He was so inspired that he wanted to
> add a harmonic acoustic guitar part. It was pure frosting on the cake. We
> used one of the newly re-strung Martins to play the part and somehow got
> the idea to double the part.

'('Silver Springs') has some of the best guitar work on the album, speaking
for what I was able to contribute to it', Buckingham says. 'A lot of layering
and volume pedals, textures across the top, and acoustic picking.'

Nicks also re-recorded her lead vocals for 'Silver Springs'. Supplementary
organ and guitar were added to 'Go Your Own Way': the offbeat guitar
acoustic riffs that lift the arrangement, and which Lindsey Buckingham
studiously taught roadie Ray Lindsey to play in concert. Sessions
concluded, the band prepared for five weeks of live concert dates.

Summer Tour

From 15 June to 28 July, Fleetwood Mac once again played a series of
concerts across the US. From California to Missouri, Nebraska, Iowa,
Michigan, Wisconsin, Illinois, Minnesota, North Dakota, Ohio and North
Carolina. The band performed four of these gigs on a triple-bill with The
Eagles and Boz Scaggs, and another with The Beach Boys and Santana.

Jeff Porcaro, who had recorded with Steely Dan and was one of the
most highly-regarded professional musicians of the 1970s and 1980s, was
the drummer in Boz Scaggs band at this time. Porcaro would watch Mick
Fleetwood from the side of the stage, intrigued by his unorthodox playing.

'I noticed Jeff sitting at the side of the stage watching me. For the entire
set', Fleetwood recalls. 'It rattled me, but I played through it. Eventually, I
forgot he was there. Then, sometime during the third week of the tour, he
came to my dressing room.'

Porcaro: 'I've watched you. I've tried to understand it. Nothing you do
up there makes sense, but it sounds beautiful. What's your method? What
are you doing in that last fill of 'Go Your Own Way'? I can't figure it out!

I've been watching every night. What do you do in the last measure on that last beat? Is the snare ahead or behind? Is the hi-hat off beat by two-quarters or is it a little more than that?'.

'Oh fuck, really…' Fleetwood responded. 'I have no idea. No idea at all.'

Porcaro founded the hugely successful band, Toto, in 1977. He died, aged 38, in 1992.

Miami Sessions and Back to Hollywood

Fleetwood Mac performed at Tampa Stadium in Florida on 4 July 1976 – a bicentennial celebration on a bill that included The Eagles and Loggins and Messina. Immediately afterwards, they spent a week at Criteria Studios in nearby Miami for further work on *Rumours*, adding polish to 'Silver Springs', 'Go Your Own Way' and 'Dreams'. The tour continued for the rest of the month, to be followed by a further three weeks of recording sessions at Wally Heider's and at a nearby studio called Davlen Sound, principally to add a $40,000 Bösendorfer grand piano to 'Don't Stop', 'You Make Loving Fun' and 'Oh, Daddy', and layered, luxurious and very beautiful backing vocals to several songs.

It was during these sessions that 'Think About It' was finally dropped.

Fleetwood Mac hits #1

The last leg of their tour to promote *Fleetwood Mac* – the final six dates of 128 – focused on California and included four concerts at the 5,000-capacity Universal Amphitheatre in Los Angeles.

In September 1976, the relentless touring and three hit singles finally pushed *Fleetwood Mac* to the top of the *Billboard* album charts, splitting a nine-week run by the ubiquitous *Frampton Comes Alive!* It skipped around the top half of the album charts for over 80 weeks, and at that time, was Warners' all-time best selling album.

Their previous highest chart position was number 34 for *Heroes are Hard to Find*. From consistently selling around 250,000 copies of their early-1970s albums – 'enough to pay Warners' electricity bill', as Mick Fleetwood put it – Fleetwood Mac had hit the big time. And *Rumours* would soon be finished…

Exit 'Silver Springs'

Further sessions for *Rumours* took place at Wally Heider's in September 1976. 'Silver Springs', more than eight-minutes-long, was edited to 4:33 but was still too long to fit on the album. Ken Caillat:

('Silver Springs') was always meant to be a part of *Rumours*, but because of space issues on vinyl, it couldn't fit on the original record.

As a replacement, Fleetwood, Buckingham and the McVies recorded the backing track for an older song, 'I Don't Want To Know', in a single session at Wally Heider's, without Stevie Nicks' involvement.

'They didn't even ask me', she said later. 'I was told in the parking lot after it had already been done.'

She confronted Mick Fleetwood, asking why 'Silver Springs' had been dropped in favour of 'I Don't Want To Know':

He said, 'There's a lot of reasons, but because basically, it's just too long. And we think that there's another of your songs that's better, so that's what we want to do'. Before I started to get upset about 'Silver Springs', I said, 'What other song?', and he said, 'A song called 'I Don't Want To Know'. And I said, 'But I don't want that song on this record', and he said, 'Well, then don't sing it'. And then I started to scream bloody murder and probably said every horribly mean thing that you could possibly say to another human being and walked back in the studio completely flipped-out. I said, 'Well, I'm not gonna sing "I Don't Want To Know" ... I am one-fifth of this band'. And they said, 'You can either (a) take a hike, or (b) you better go out there and sing 'I Don't Want To Know' or you're only gonna have two songs on the record'. And so, basically, with a gun to my head, I went out and sang 'I Don't Want To Know'. And they put 'Silver Springs' on the back of 'Go Your Own Way'. That always put a shadow over 'I Don't Want To Know'. Even though I love it and it came out great.

Mick Fleetwood:

'I Don't Want To Know' often gets forgotten about in terms of it being part of *Rumours*. I think it's really unique. You get those voices together. And that was their style.... what they brought into this thing called Fleetwood Mac. Everything else grew from around that.

'I know Stevie was disappointed that 'Silver Springs' didn't make it at the time', comments Lindsey Buckingham. 'We were worried a bit about the flow of the album and what the album needed. It was a shame that it didn't make it. It was certainly warranted.'

Never Break The Chain

Fleetwood Mac moved to the Record Plant in Los Angeles for a final set of recording sessions for *Rumours*. It was here that they finally turned their attention back to Christine McVie's song, 'Keep Me There' – the first song recorded for the album, eleven months before. Ken Caillat:

> It had sat around for quite a while and none of us felt good about it. We all knew that it had potential – it certainly had a great tag, but the chorus was only okay. We needed something equally special for the first half, something that would unite the band and heal their wounds, something written by the whole band for the very first time.

The end result was 'The Chain'. If Fleetwood Mac had recorded just this one song, then their legend would be secure. Mick Fleetwood:

> 'The Chain' was very much a band composition. Originally we had no words to it. And it really only became a song when Stevie wrote some. She walked in one day and said, 'I've written some words that might be good for that thing you were doing in the studio the other day'. So it was put together. Lindsey arranged and made a song out of all the bits and pieces that we were putting down onto tape. And then, once it was arranged and we knew what we were doing, we went in and recorded it. The riff is John McVie's contribution – a major contribution because that bass line is still being played on British TV in the car-racing series to this day. The Grand Prix thing. It was really something that just came out of us playing in the studio. But it ultimately becomes a band thing anyway, because we all have so much of our own individual style, our own stamp that makes the sound of Fleetwood Mac: what you do, and what you feel when we're all making music together, is what Fleetwood Mac ends up being.

Ken Caillat: 'What was the best day of your life? And did you know it when you were living it? That's what it was like watching 'The Chain' go down'. Lindsay Buckingham later told *Rolling Stone*:

> There's one track on the album that started out as one song in Sausalito. We decided it needed a bridge, so we cut a bridge and edited it into the rest of the song. We didn't get a vocal and left it for a long time in a bunch of pieces. It almost went off the album. Then we listened back and decided we liked the bridge but didn't like the rest of the song. I came in one day,

and said why don't we just remove the verses? And we can do some sort of measurement of what the tape is and do a reverse count back from there to create a metronome to play to, and once we have the blank tape in, we can figure out what we want to put in there! Mick or I laid down the kick drum that gave us a start point. Eventually, I started fooling with the dobro, and that became the foundation for what was written over that. The three-part harmony of 'Listen to the wind blow' was a collaboration of the three writers. We saved the ending. The ending was the only thing left from the original track. We ended up calling it 'The Chain' because it was a bunch of pieces.

Buckingham added a folky dobro introduction lifted directly from his own song 'Lola (My Love)', recorded for *Buckingham Nicks*. Ken Caillat:

Finally, everything clicked. 'The Chain' changed drastically over the course of a year, but there was something about it that always made people think it was worth coming back to.

The entire album was mixed at the Record Plant. Some final overdubs took place there, such as percussion and vibraphone on 'Dreams' and lead guitar on 'Go Your Own Way'.
   The final mix of 'Go Your Own Way' takes sections of several guitar solos. You can hear the transitions at 2:53 and 3:14. Buckingham would later have to learn to play the solo the way Caillat had edited his different takes together.
   Several sets of backing vocals would be recorded. Ken Caillat:

I remember when we were doing background vocals, Stevie and Lindsey were having an argument. Vicious name-calling – 'you motherfucker' this, 'you fucking bastard' that. Back and forth it went. The tape would start rolling and they'd sing, 'Yooooooou make loving fun', just beautiful, two little angels. The tape would stop and they'd be calling each other names again. They didn't miss a beat.

'Gold Dust Woman' was given a new lead vocal track. Cris Morris, who was a recording assistant on these sessions, explained in *Q* magazine: 'Stevie was very passionate about getting that vocal right. It seemed like it was directed straight at Lindsey, and she was letting it all out. She worked right through the night on it, and finally did it after loads of takes'.

Ken Caillat says:

The song grew more evil as we built it. I called over to (local hire company)
SIR, and they send over a bunch of weird instruments, (including) a
harpsichord. It could be amplified. When you do this, it begins to sound
very bright and edgy. We initially thought that Christine would play (it), but
because of the difficulty with timing that instrument, we decided that we
should have Mick play it so that we could take advantage of his intuitive feel
to get those wild sounds right. The good news was that Mick had a great feel
for the timing. The bad news was that he didn't know how to play a piano.
We decided that the best sound from the harpsichord wouldn't come from
playing chords. Instead, we wanted single notes, stabbed throughout the
song. Mick stood over the keyboard, randomly hitting the keys at the timing
he desired. Finally, we decided to mark all of the correct keys with a piece
of black tape so that all Mick had to do was hit one of the pieces of tape,
which would make the track sound much better. When we ran the song
through the phaser, it added an effect like a giant wah-wah pedal, but with
many random and constantly changing sounds. Listen for its effects at 0:09,
0:25 and 0:28 seconds. You'll hear exactly what the mighty phaser does. We
weren't looking for musicality; we were looking for accents, mood.

**And then, the sound of breaking glass. Buckingham's then-girlfriend Carol
Ann Harris:**

"Gold Dust Woman' needs something', Lindsey announced through the
smoke. 'It's not atmospheric enough'. So… we brought some sheets of
glass and set up microphones in the parking lot. We want to record the
sound of splintering glass and work it into the song. Mick's eyes fired up
with a devilish gleam. He rubbed his hands together, fiendishly. 'I want
to be the one who gets to crash the glass! Me, me! I'm the tallest! I'm the
best glass-breaker in the friggin' world! Let's do it!'. He scampered into
the rain with Richard by his side. I stayed in the control room with Lindsey
and listened to the hysteria from the parking lot booming through the
huge speakers in the room. It took Richard five minutes to stop Mick
from laughing, but once he did, the sound of breaking, shattering glass
was recorded. The finished version of 'Gold Dust Woman' begins with an
unearthly tinkling that sounds dark and ominous. It changed the whole
vibe of the song. This was the first of many times that I'd see Lindsey's
genius at work.

Ken Caillat says:

Stevie had a lot of Courvoisier in her and she did this incredible coyote-like howling at the end. She had become this witch she was always writing about. To accentuate her vocals, Mick went into this room we had mic'd up, and he broke sheets of glass. He was wearing goggles and coveralls – it was pretty funny. He just went mad, bashing glass with this big hammer. He tried to do it on cue, but it was difficult. Eventually, we said, 'Just break the glass', and we fit it all in'.

New radio mixes of the lead single 'Go Your Own Way' and 'Silver Springs' were made at Wally Heider's in late November, and the entire album was mixed at the Producers' Workshop in Los Angeles in December 1976 and January 1977. Finally, the album was finished. Ken Caillat:

So, on January 4, 1977, 24 days short of a year since the day I had left home to start this wonderful, exhausting, life-changing adventure, our songs were mixed and sequenced. I made copies of the final album for everyone in the band so that they could take a cassette home and listen until their hearts were content.

1977

Rumours Is Released
Fleetwood Mac's eleventh studio album was released in February 1977.

Why is this easy-listening rock different from all other easy-listening rock, give or take an ancient harmony or two? Because myths of love lost and found are less invidious (at least in rock and roll) than myths of the road? Because the cute-voiced woman writes and sings the tough lyrics and the husky-voiced woman the vulnerable ones? Because they've got three melodist-vocalists on the job? Because Mick Fleetwood and John McVie learned their rhythm licks playing blues? Because they stuck to this beguiling formula when it barely broke even? Because this album is both more consistent and more eccentric than its blockbuster predecessor? Plus, it jumps right out of the speakers at you?
(**Robert Christgau**, *Village Voice*, 1977)

Each tune, each phrase regains its raw, immediate emotional power – which is why *Rumours* touched a nerve upon its 1977 release and has since transcended its era to be one of the greatest, most compelling pop albums of all time.
(**Stephen Thomas Erlewine**, *AllMusic*)

Ken Caillat:

The moment I knew that *Rumours* was big, I had just gotten into my car and turned my radio on. The DJ said, 'Boy have I got a treat for you, I'm going to play you the new Fleetwood Mac album, and wait till you hear how great it sounds!'. My heart leaped into my chest and then he played 'Go Your Own Way'. He was right, it sounded so good, you can't imagine how proud I was!

Rock and roll has this bad habit of being unpredictable. You never can tell when a band will undergo that alchemic transmigration from lead to gold. The medium of transformation is almost always a hit single, but such turnarounds often swamp a band in notoriety it can't live up to. But in Fleetwood Mac's case, the departure of guitarist, Bob Welch, amounted to the biggest break they ever had. With that and the addition of Lindsey Buckingham and Stevie Nicks, Fleetwood Mac suddenly became a California pop group; instead of laborious blues/rock jams, they started turning out bright little three-minute singles with a hook in every chorus. Fleetwood Mac has finally realized the apotheosis of that early-Sixties blues crusade to get back to the roots. It's just that it took a couple of Californians and a few lessons from The Byrds, Buffalo Springfield and The Eagles to get there.

(John Swenson, *Rolling Stone*, 21 April 1977)

Gossip alone would not have made *Rumours* such a wildly successful album. It's the unique chemistry in Fleetwood Mac and the craftsmanship in songwriting and production that makes *Rumours* the most perfect pop album of all time. *Rumours* brought together English and American musicians from different schools – the blues and pop. It had strong lyrics written and performed by both men and women, three exceptional singers, plus the sonic ambition of Lindsey Buckingham, the fluid inventiveness of a great rhythm section, and unlimited resources to make a totally state-of-the-art album.

(Toby Cresswell and Craig Mathieson, *The 100 Best Albums of All Time*, 2013)

Rumours has been re-released three times. The 2004 'remastered edition' adds 'Silver Springs' and a second disc of 'Roughs and Outtakes, Early Demos, and Jam Sessions'. These include demos for 'Planet Of The Universe' and 'Doesn't Anything Last', the incomplete 'Think About It', the first version of 'Keep It There', and a couple of inessential jams. A massive 2012 box set includes both discs from the 2004 version and adds two further CDs (more outtakes and newly remixed live performances from 1977), a DVD and a vinyl reproduction of the original album. Those fans with shallower pockets could opt for the three-CD version which includes the remastered album and the two newly-produced bonus CDs. A further 'deluxe edition' released in 2019 is the same as the 2012 multi-disc box set, but without the DVD or vinyl album. *Rumours* would re-enter the *Billboard* charts in October 2020, spurred on by 30.6 million streams of the album's songs, from publicity generated by a viral TikTok video, set to 'Dreams'.

The Rumours Tour
Fleetwood Mac started rehearsals for their most important tour to date in February 1977 at a small studio called Rat, in the San Fernando Valley.

Tapes of those rehearsals circulate between collectors. Dipping into the band's back catalogue, both 'Tell Me All The Things You Do' and 'Believe Me' were worked up, but the former was performed infrequently, if at all. Stevie Nicks was absent for some of these rehearsals, and Christine McVie filled in singing 'Dreams', 'Rhiannon', 'Landslide' and 'Gold Dust Woman'. The lack of audio quality is eclipsed by the rarity of these performances.

Mick Fleetwood: 'We hit the road playing a powerhouse set that consisted of hits from both albums, selling out arenas from ten to fifteen thousand'.

Those songs often had a harder edge in concert. 'Rhiannon' would be transformed into an eight-minute epic, and 'World Turning' would lengthen and expand, sometimes lasting up to twenty minutes. 'I'm So Afraid' started its transformation to the show-stopper of 1979-1980. Roadie Ray Lindsey, added rhythm guitar to the songs 'Monday Morning', 'Go Your Own Way' and 'Second Hand News'.

Production rehearsals were held at Soundstage B of SIR Studios on Sunset Boulevard in Los Angeles. A wonderful full run-through recording includes 'Say You Love Me', 'Go Your Own Way', 'Believe Me', 'Dreams', 'The Chain', 'Why?', 'Landslide', 'Never Going Back Again', 'You Make Loving Fun', 'I'm So Afraid', 'Oh Daddy', 'Gold Dust Woman', 'Oh Well', 'World Turning' and 'Rhiannon' – about as perfect a setlist as you could ask for from this period of the band.

> Fleetwood Mac kicks off their 1977 tour with a benefit for the Jacques Cousteau Society at the Berkeley Community Theater. Except for a short film about penguins (long a symbol of Fleetwood Mac), the band is the only act on the bill. Material from their just-released *Rumours* LP is met with as much applause of recognition as songs from their previous album, which garnered three hit singles. Midway through the show it becomes apparent that vocalist Stevie Nicks, battling a strained throat, is not going to be able to make it through the set. The spotlight turns to the band's other two songwriters, Christine McVie and, more noticeably, Lindsey Buckingham, who displays a degree of confidence and guitar technique barely hinted at on album. The concert climaxes near the end, with Buckingham's dramatic 'I'm So Afraid' taken a bit slower than the recorded version.
> (*Musician*, June 1981)

Back to Europe
After a date at the Kemper Arena, Kansas City, Missouri, on 1 April 1977, the band flew overnight for a tour of the UK, starting in Birmingham, the

very next night after their Kansas City concert. It was their first British tour since 1973. By now, the band's set consisted almost entirely of songs from *Fleetwood Mac* and *Rumours*: typically 'Don't Stop', 'The Chain', 'Monday Morning', 'Dreams', 'Rhiannon', 'Why?', 'Landslide', 'Never Going Back Again', 'Over My Head', 'Gold Dust Woman', 'Oh Well', 'Silver Springs', 'You Make Loving Fun', 'I'm So Afraid', 'Say You Love Me', 'World Turning' and 'Go Your Own Way'. Concerts would now close with Christine McVie alone on stage singing 'Songbird'.

Rumours hit the number one spot in the US on 2 April 1977, spending a total of 31 weeks there over the next nine months, with four separate runs at the top. This is still the record number of weeks at the head of the *Billboard* best-selling albums list for a duo or group. At its height in America, *Rumours* was going platinum – one million sales – every thirty days. It sold ten million copies within a year of its release and ultimately went on to sell 25 million copies. Until the release of *Thriller*, Fleetwood Mac's eleventh long-player was the best-selling album of all time. Even now, 40-plus years on, only seven albums have sold more copies than *Rumours*: *Thriller*, *Back in Black*, *Bat Out of Hell*, *The Dark Side of the Moon*, *The Bodyguard OST*, *Eagles Greatest Hits 1971-1975* and *Saturday Night Fever*.

After their first of three dates at the Rainbow in London, 8 April 1977, the group were visited backstage by Peter Green. They also met up with Danny Kirwan. Both men were struggling with mental issues. This was the last time that Mick Fleetwood saw Danny Kirwan. A few days later, Fleetwood Mac performed at Palais de Sport in Paris. Live versions of 'Don't Stop' and 'Dreams' from this concert were released on *Fleetwood Mac Live* in 1980. The tour continued to Germany, France and Sweden, then back to the US for another three months of live dates between May and July. The warhorse 'Why?' was finally dropped.

Some of the line-ups from these summer concerts would make fans of classic rock drool today. On 1 May 1977, the Folsom Music Festival in Bolder, Colorado, drew 61,500 fans. Fleetwood Mac headlined, with sets by Bob Seger and The Silver Bullet Band, Firefall, John Sebastian, and Country Joe McDonald. A week later, the 'Day on the Green' in Oakland, CA hosted Fleetwood Mac, The Doobie Brothers and Gary Wright. At the end of the month, the Tangerine Bowl in Orlando, Florida, promoted the Rock Superbowl with Fleetwood Mac, Bob Seger and the Silver Bullet Band, Return to Forever and Kenny Loggins. A few days later in New Orleans, Fleetwood Mac, Seger and Loggins, were joined by Foreigner promoting their debut album and new single 'Cold As Ice'.

French Kiss and 'Werewolves of London'

During a break in the tour, Buckingham, Fleetwood and Chris McVie helped former bandmate, Bob Welch, re-record his song 'Sentimental Lady' – first released on *Bare Trees* – for his solo album, *French Kiss*. This new version was a top ten hit for Welch when it was released as a single in September 1977.

At around this time, Mick Fleetwood and John McVie supplied drums and bass to Warren Zevon's classic single, 'Werewolves Of London', recorded at the Sound Factory in Los Angeles with co-producer, guitarist and future Stevie Nicks musical director, Waddy Wachtel.

It is perhaps coincidence that the opening moments of Stevie Nicks' 'Angel' – from *Tusk* (recorded in April 1979) – sound 'very much' like 'Werewolves Of London'. And although the I-VII-IV chord progression is familiar from songs such as 'Sympathy For The Devil', 'Gloria' and 'Sweet Home Alabama', the home key (D) and Fleetwood and McVie's rhythm parts are identical in both 'Werewolves Of London' and 'Angel'. Even the beats-per-minute are very close, with 'Werewolves..' at 104 and 'Angel' at 112.

US Tour

Fleetwood Mac toured the US again from mid-August to early October, including three nights at The Forum in Los Angeles.

Carol Ann Harris wrote:

Fleetwood Mac returned home to play The Forum. It was the biggest venue in the city and it was completely sold out. The acoustics were fabulous, and playing in it was like being on the cover of Rolling Stone. If you sold out The Forum, you'd 'arrived' in the music industry. The band was to play to an audience of over 19,000 fans (each night) and they were feeling completely, insanely freaked. It wasn't the size of the audience that had them on the edge of a nervous breakdown: it was the simple, brutal fact that in L.A. they would be playing in front of their musical peers – rock giants like Bruce Springsteen, Tom Petty, Don Henley, David Bowie, Mick Jagger: any or all of them could be sitting in the audience. It didn't really matter who you were or how much commercial success you had in the record industry, playing in front of people whose opinion matters to you – and who are themselves your musical idols – was a recipe for high-octane stress. There was definitely a sense of menace in Lindsey's glare, and I winced as I watched him break a string on his guitar during 'World

Turning', curse at (roadie) Ray Lindsey, and almost throw the guitar at him. As I watched and listened to Lindsey play like he was possessed by a demon, I knew that that night's show was one of the best the band had ever played.

Studio D

Rumours' protracted recording sessions had resulted in Fleetwood Mac using five different studios in three different cities before they got exactly what they wanted. For its follow-up, Mick Fleetwood decided that the band should build their own studio. A state-of-the-art facility called Studio D was constructed at The Village Recorder in Los Angeles between September 1977 and June 1978. The final bill ran to about $1.4 million.

Such was the deal struck that Fleetwood Mac did not own the studio and still had to rent recording time. Considerable amounts of money were spent on perks such as a lounge with Dutch beer on tap and huge ivory tusks on each side of the console.

To New Zealand, Australia and Japan

They had just ten days at home between the end of the US tour and the band's first trip to Oceania and Japan. During this time, Mick Fleetwood started an affair with Stevie Nicks.

John McVie: 'Mick and Stevie? I never knew. Never. Didn't have a clue. Not an inkling. And I still don't want to know. That was completely their business'.

'Never in a million years could you have told me that would happen. That was the biggest surprise. But Mick is definitely one of my great, great loves', Nicks was still claiming years later. 'But that really wasn't good for anybody. Everybody was angry, because Mick was married to a wonderful girl and had two wonderful children. I was horrified. I loved these people. I loved his family. So it couldn't possibly work out. And it didn't. It just couldn't.'

Fleetwood Mac performed in Auckland, Brisbane, Sydney, Melbourne, Queensland, Perth and Adelaide, then flew to Japan for four concerts. These Japanese dates were filmed, and two of these – Osaka on 4 December and the following night in Tokyo – were broadcast on the radio.

'I hired a crew to travel with us', Mick Fleetwood said later, 'giving them free rein to capture us both onstage and off. My intention was to edit the film and release it as a feature to run in cinemas. That never happened'.

Footage that has leaked to YouTube over the years shows the strength of this line-up: especially Nicks' charisma, Buckingham's considerable skills (and sheer drive) as a guitarist, and, of course, the power of one of the greatest rhythm sections the world has ever seen. The version of 'The Chain' from Tokyo may well be the best ever recording by this version of Fleetwood Mac.

The performance of 'Monday Morning' – recorded on 5 December 1977 at Nippon Budokan, Tokyo – would be released on *Fleetwood Mac Live* and as the B-side of the UK version of 'The Farmer's Daughter' (both in 1980).

1977 ended with dates at the Royal Lahaina Tennis Stadium in Honolulu and the Maui Sheraton. Three years of solid graft had placed Fleetwood Mac at the very pinnacle of their profession. Next... how to follow-up the biggest selling album of all time?

Lindsay Buckingham:

We had this album which was so huge it was disproportionate from the music. It became not even about the music at some point. It became about success. It became about the voyeurism that we were bringing out in people, in terms of them sort of looking into our personal lives and the fact that the songs were about what was going on with us as people. So it became this phenomenon which (was) somehow detached from the music. We were probably poised for *Rumours II*. I don't know how you do that, but somehow my light bulb that went off was, 'Let's not do that. Let's very pointedly not do that'.

1978

Grammy Winners

Fleetwood Mac took a break for the first four months of 1978. On 4 January 1978, Peter Green married Jane Samuel at Mick Fleetwood's Los Angeles home. At the end of January, *Rumours* finally reached number 1 in the UK, in its 50th consecutive week on the chart. The 20th Annual Grammy Awards were held on 23 February 1978 at the Shrine Auditorium in Los Angeles and were broadcast live on American television. They were hosted by John Denver. Fleetwood Mac were awarded Album of the Year for *Rumours.* Three weeks later on 18 March, Stevie Nicks and Mick Fleetwood joined Bob Welch on stage at the second California Jam, held at the Ontario Motor Speedway. They performed 'Ebony Eyes' together, as part of a bill that included Aerosmith, Foreigner, Ted Nugent, Dave Mason, Santana and Heart.

During this period, Buckingham and Nicks co-produced *Not Shy*: the second album by American singer, Walter Egan. Buckingham and Nicks' harmonies are unmistakable in the chorus of the top ten hit song, 'Magnet and Steel'. Buckingham also sang and played on a cover of Jackson Browne's 'Something Fine' from Leo Sayer's self-titled sixth album, released that September. Nicks recorded a duet called 'Whenever I Call You Friend' with Kenny Loggins, which would enter the *Billboard* top five later in the year.

Samuel Graham's book, *Fleetwood Mac, The Authorised History*, was published by Warner Bros. Publications in 1978. It's a surprisingly honest and open account of the band's first ten years together and includes interviews with the five band members, as well as Peter Green and Bob Welch.

Tusk

Personnel:
Lindsey Buckingham: vocals, guitars, bass guitar, keyboards, drums, percussion
Mick Fleetwood: drums, percussion
Christine McVie: vocals, keyboards, piano, organ
John McVie: bass guitar
Stevie Nicks: vocals
with
Peter Green: guitar (on 'Brown Eyes')
USC Trojan Marching Band 'The Spirit of Troy': horns and percussion (on 'Tusk')

Recorded July 1978 to September 1979 at the Village Recorder, Los Angeles, and Lindsey Buckingham's home studio, June Street, Los Angeles.
Produced by Fleetwood Mac, Richard Dashut and Ken Caillat.
Album release: October 1979.
Highest chart placings: UK: 1, US: 4
Side one: 'Over And Over', 'The Ledge', 'Think About Me', 'Save Me A Place', 'Sara'
Side two: 'What Makes You Think You're The One', 'Storms', 'That's All For Everyone', 'Not That Funny', 'Sisters Of The Moon'
Side three: 'Angel', 'That's Enough For Me', 'Brown Eyes' (alternative version on 25 Years – The Chain), 'Never Make Me Cry', 'I Know I'm Not Wrong'
Side four: 'Honey Hi', 'Beautiful Child' (alternative mix on 25 Years – The Chain), 'Walk A Thin Line', 'Tusk' (alternative mix on 25 Years – The Chain), 'Never Forget'

'Tusk' b/w 'Never Make You Cry'
US and UK single releases September 1979 (highest US chart position: 8; highest UK chart position: 6)

'Sara' b/w 'That's Enough For Me'
US and UK single releases in December 1979 (highest US chart position: 7; highest UK chart position: 37). Single mix of 'Sara' on 50 Years – Don't Stop.

'Not That Funny' b/w 'Think About Me'
UK single releases: March 1980 (did not chart)

'Think About Me' b/w 'Save Me A Place'
US single release: March 1980 of (highest chart position: 20)

'Sisters Of The Moon' b/w 'Walk A Thin Line'
UK single release June 1980 (highest chart position: 86)

After a period renting Joe Walsh's house on Mulholland Drive in Los Angeles in spring 1978, and with three weeks before they were due to head on tour, Fleetwood Mac reconvened on 24 June 1978 – Mick Fleetwood's 31st birthday – at the new Studio D, to record their next album and follow-up to their biggest seller.

'Lindsey was hell-bent that this album would be nothing like *Rumours*', Steve Nicks said later.

'*Tusk* was a radical departure!' recalls Ken Caillat. 'When Lindsey showed up at the studio the first day he had cut all his hair off, we all looked at each other and said, 'Oh, oh'. I believe Lindsey did not know where he wanted to go from here; the Eagles annoyed him in that they never change their musical approach, and he wanted Fleetwood Mac's to change. He thought Fleetwood Mac should continue growing musically. And so *Tusk* was born'.

'(Sessions) lasted thirteen months', said Christine McVie, 'and it took every bit of inner strength we had. It was very hard on us, like being a hostage in Iran, and to an extent, Lindsey was the Ayatollah'.

This first session initially concentrated on assessing demo recordings. Nicks brought 'Storms' and 'Sisters Of The Moon', and McVie put forward 'Brown Eyes' and 'Over And Over'. Not surprisingly, 'Storms' hit a sore spot for Lindsey Buckingham. Carol Ann Harris:

> Stevie had brought in one of her songs with melody and lyrics already laid down over a simple basic track. To me it already sounded great. But not good enough, apparently, for Lindsey. Stevie, standing in the middle of the room, kept a serene smile on her face as the band listened to 'Storms'. As the last note faded away, she looked around the room, waiting for the positive comments and feedback that she obviously felt the song would garner from everyone present. And then it all started to turn ugly. By the time Lindsey was finished dissecting everything in detail about what was wrong with the song, he smiled serenely and said, 'I like it, Stevie. It just needs some work, that's all'. As Stevie listened to Lindsey's comments. You could almost see the steam coming off her. Added to the weight of the battle scars from Lindsey's and Stevie's past personal relationship, they made the atmosphere of the studio even uglier with each passing day.

Buckingham was more interested in his song 'The Ledge', at that time called 'Can't Walk Out Of Here'.

'The (demo) cassette was distorted, and I thought 'Yikes – that sounds horrible'', recalls co-producer, Ken Caillat. Seven takes of 'Can't Walk Out Of Here' were recorded, none to the composer's satisfaction. A version of a Chris McVie song called 'Come On, Baby' was also attempted, but its composer was unhappy with the lyrics. The recording was left incomplete for now.

'Lindsay's Song #1' – later called 'I Know I'm Not Wrong' – was also worked on. Versions of these three songs taken from the June 1978 sessions would be released on the 2015 expanded version of *Tusk*. Buckingham would continue developing 'I Know I'm Not Wrong' – demo recordings from August 1978, October 1978, November 1978, January 1979 and April 1979 have been officially released. The January 1979 version, with overdubs, is the version released on *Tusk*.

Penguin Country Summer Safari

After production rehearsals at SIR in Hollywood, Fleetwood Mac would undertake a stadium tour of thirteen US cities in July and August 1978: the last leg of a tour that had started eighteen months earlier. Nicks' song, 'Sisters Of The Moon' received its live debut on this tour. On several dates, Fleetwood Mac shared the bill with their former guitarist, Bob Welch, including for some of their largest audiences ever, at the JFK Stadium in Philadelphia on 29 and 30 July.

Nearly 65,000 fans braved threatening skies July 29, to get a look at this wildly successful recording act at the hulking, antiquated football stadium best known as the home of the Army-Navy game. Unlike the Rolling Stones date held here earlier in the summer, the afternoon passed without major incident, as the crowd was good-natured and orderly. The band hit the stage about 4:20 and immediately brought the throng to its feet as it opened with some of its stronger up-tempo material. Instrumentally the band was in rare form throughout, with drummer Mick Fleetwood giving a particularly strong performance. Fleetwood combines the creativity and taste of a veteran jazz drummer with the power and flair of a rocker. His solid time-keeping and spirited fills are one of the group's greatest yet most appreciated (sic) assets. Unfortunately, vocalist Stevie Nicks was in poor form as she seemed unable to get her voice to do the things it does on record. This was particularly disappointing to her fans, since Nicks is the voice featured on some of the group's biggest hits, such as 'Rhiannon' and 'Dreams'. For the most part, the band's seventeen-song, 100-minute set was well-paced, with the group spreading its strongest material – such as 'Listen To The Wind Blow' (sic), 'Oh Daddy', 'Say You Love Me' and 'You Make Loving Fun' – throughout the show. The set did get tedious toward the end, with 'You Can Go Your Own Way' being the only song in the last six that held the crowd's attention.

(Robert Ford, *Billboard* Magazine, 12 August 1978)

The final date of the tour – 30 August 1978 in Baton Rouge – would be Fleetwood Mac's last live show for fourteen months. The concert was recorded and broadcast by WLBP-FM.

Back to Tusk: 'Never Forget', 'Sisters Of The Moon', 'Brown Eyes'

With the tour over, the band headed back to Studio D.

Christine McVie later admitted: 'Recording *Tusk* was quite absurd. The studio contract rider for refreshments was like a telephone directory. Exotic food delivered to the studio, crates of champagne. And it had to be the best, with no thought of what it cost. Stupid. Really stupid. Somebody once said that with the money we spent on champagne on one night, they could have made an entire album. And it's probably true.

Carol Ann Harris:

Playing it safe, Fleetwood Mac had decided to record (some of) Christine's and Stevie's songs first. This allowed the five of them to settle back into being a band working on a common cause, instead of separate musicians who were fighting and clawing at each other over radical artistic differences. Lindsey was brilliant when it came to contributing vocals, musical ideas, harmonies, and guitar parts to the music of both of the women in the band. I was quickly learning that one of Lindsey's biggest talents was the ability to act as a producer on another artist's music. He seemed to know inherently what a song needed, and his song arrangements proved it. And despite his vow that this time around, he didn't want to use his best ideas on Stevie's or Christine's songs, he now appeared to be willing to contribute whatever he felt their music needed. Within a month, Fleetwood Mac had seemingly put aside all differences – for now – and music was actually starting to be recorded.

Christine McVie's 'Never Forget' had started as 'Come On, Baby' in June 1978. With re-written lyrics, a new version combined finger-picked acoustic guitar and Hammond B3. Harmony backing vocals were added later.

Stevie Nicks' 'Sisters Of The Moon' was originally a piano/vocal demo.

'I honestly don't know what the hell this song is about', Nicks said. 'It wasn't a love song, it wasn't written about a man. ... It was just about a feeling I might have had over a couple of days, going inward in my gnarly trollness. Makes no sense. Perfect for this record.'

Once again, John McVie and Mick Fleetwood were in perfect sync. Thirty-six takes were recorded in total to realise Nicks' mystic vision. Stevie and Christine later added the coven of howling witches; Lindsey Buckingham provided distorted Fender Stratocaster.

'Brown Eyes' is a song for Dennis Wilson, Christine McVie's then-current beau. It was recorded by the full band, with added electric piano, guitars and sixteen tracks of vocals. A few weeks later, a stellar guitar part would be added by Peter Green. This can be heard in the fade-out. A different mix on the expanded version of *Tusk* includes much more of Green's work.

'Lindsey's Song #2'
Carol Ann Harris:

Over the summer, Lindsey had ordered a reel-to-reel portable recording machine with a mixer and speakers – the works – to be built into three large anvil cases on wheels. Once set up, it spanned seven feet and stood three feet high. Lindsey loved it. He'd already started to work on new songs for the next album. Every night off that we'd had so far, he spent recording. Sitting cross-legged on the floor, with his guitar in front of the red anvil cases of his portable studio, he laid songs down on tape, as a cloud of smoke from an ever-present joint, hovered around his head. One of the first songs that he wrote was 'That's All For Everyone', which was about loneliness and a man's search for someone or someplace in which to find refuge.

'That's All For Everyone' (aka 'Lindsay's Song #2') started as an instrumental demo, and ended as 100% Beach Boys with triple-tracked lead vocals, lush reverb and echo. Recorded initially as a band performance, gradually all of the instruments were replaced to include new drums, bass and piano parts (played by Buckingham), an African thumb piano, maracas and, famously, the highly compressed sound of Kleenex boxes.

The instrumental demo is available on the 2004 reissue of *Tusk*. An early mix from 20 October 1978 can be heard on the 2015 reissue of *Tusk:* this is quite different but equally brilliant. A remix of the final version – with even more reverb – is also included on this same set.

'Storms', 'Beautiful Child', 'Over and Over', 'Honey Hi'
Stevie Nicks' second contribution was her song for Mick: 'Storms'.
She said:

Every night he will break your heart
I should've known from the first

I'd be the broken-hearted
But I loved you from the start
Not all the prayers in the world could save us

The basic track was Lindsey Buckingham's acoustic guitar – later replaced by a nylon-stringed guitar – with overdubs of Hammond B3, electric piano, upright bass and floor toms.

'Beautiful Child' is a luscious Stevie Nicks ballad with the rare (for *Tusk*) group harmony vocals, sung one voice at a time in the studio's echo chamber. She admitted in 2013 that the lyrics were about a recent affair with former Beatles publicist, Derek Taylor.

'It didn't last very long because he was married', Nicks said, 'but it affected me very much'.

'Over And Over' is a pure 1970s ballad with a beautiful slide guitar part by Lindsey Buckingham. Parts of the vocal lines were arranged with the help of Dennis Wilson. Fleetwood Mac's three singers recorded their harmonies together in the studio, and as with earlier songs such as 'Say You Love Me' and 'Don't Stop', the final build has a new hook as the song's title is repeated, well, over and over. Listen closely for Buckingham cheekily singing, 'Over 'bend' over'.

Another Christine McVie song, 'Honey Hi', would be recorded by Mick (congas), Christine (electric piano and vocals), John (bass), Lindsey (acoustic guitar) and Stevie (harmony vocals) all sitting in a circle in Studio D. Take four was the master. More vocals were overdubbed, with canon-like repeats.

By now, it was late October 1978. Fleetwood Mac had recorded nine songs: Christine McVie's 'Never Forget', 'Brown Eyes', 'Over And Over' and 'Honey Hi'; Stevie Nicks' 'Sisters Of The Moon', 'Storms' and 'Beautiful Child'; and Lindsay Buckingham's 'That's All For Everyone'.

That imbalance was about to be redressed. The remaining sessions would be dominated by the musical vision of Lindsey Buckingham, as he later recalled:

Coming off an album as successful as *(Rumours)*, we were being asked to get on this treadmill of clichéd thought and hash out the same thing again. Punk and new wave had kicked in during the meantime and, although I wasn't directly influenced by that music, it gave me a kick in the pants in terms of having the courage to try to shake things up a little bit. I wanted something that had a little more depth.

'The whole next year on *Tusk*, we were fighting all the time with him', co-producer, Ken Caillat, said. 'He actually built a studio in his house and took the tapes home so we couldn't have anything to say about them.'

'*Tusk* really grew out of him having a home studio that he really was starting to work in', says Walter Egan. 'And it was, of course, a reaction to the overblown '70s rock that was going on, and (Fleetwood Mac) were really at the centre of it.'

Buckingham had taken the June 1978 recording of 'The Ledge', adding detuned sped-up and slowed-down guitars, ultimately replacing the entire original track, with the exception of Mick Fleetwood's snare drum.

'I was trying to find things that were off the radar', Buckingham recalled of the song. 'On this, that one guitar was covering everything. It was a concept piece on that level. There was nothing for John or Christine to do.'

Later still, he would take this a step further.

'On most of his songs, he completed almost all of the basic recording in the studio at our house on June Street', Carol Ann Harris wrote. 'There were, of course, parts that needed to be recorded or backtracked in Studio D. And every single note, whether a vocal or a bass or a drum part, was done exactly to Lindsey's specifications. Standing over John as he put down a bass part on a song, Lindsey played the part for him and then insisted that he copy every note as closely as was humanly possible.'

'Well, I wasn't about to be a session player', McVie said. 'I could only play the part as I saw it. For better or for worse. As it turned out, it wasn't that bad, and you know, how hard can you argue with a writer of a song? They have their vision, and somewhere – one hopes – the two can meet.'

'Lindsey was really making a stand', Nicks said of *Tusk*.

Musician (#33, June 1981): Was the change from *Rumours* to *Tusk* a conscious attempt to not get pegged as a pop song group?
Buckingham: Well, it's really hard to say. In a way, yes. Speaking for myself, my songs are probably more of a departure than Stevie's or Christine's, but even theirs, the arrangements are slightly different. There's been little effort made to fit them into a single mold, whereas on *Rumours*, every song was more or less crafted as that kind of song. It's not that the songs on *Tusk* are long; in fact, someone asked me when the album first came out why all my songs were so short. I just said, 'Well, rock 'n' roll songs were traditionally short songs.' But, for me, it was a question of experimenting with a new format in recording. Some of those tunes were recorded in my house on my 24-track. The overall atmosphere of the album just evolved by itself.

We wanted to do a double album – I don't think we knew exactly where it was going. But I was interested in pursuing some things that were a little bit rawer. You just hear so much stuff on the radio that has the particular drum sound. I mean, everything is worked around the drums these days. It's all so studio-ized; I thought it was important to delve into some things that were off to the side a little bit more so that we're not so clichéd. And we certainly did that – at the expense of selling a few records. Between the *Fleetwood Mac* album and *Rumours*, we changed the people we were working with totally, even though *Fleetwood Mac* had sold two and a half or three million copies. We could have stuck with a good sure thing, and we went through a lot of hell re-establishing a working relationship with other people to move forward and to try to grow, which we did on the *Rumours* LP. Now on Tusk we more or less did the same thing and took a lot of chances, but we did it because it was something we felt was right to do and was important, and it shook things up. It certainly shook people's preconception of us up a bit. We divided our audience a little bit. A lot of people who were sort of on one side and saw *Rumours* as kind of MOR, were really pleased by *Tusk*; and a lot of people were very disappointed because they were expecting more of the same thing. You can't let what you think is going to sell, dictate over what you think is important.

The first songs to be recorded this way were, 'That's Enough for Me' – initially called 'Out on the Road' or 'Lindsay's Song #2' – 'Walk A Thin Line' (aka 'Song #3') and 'Save Me A Place'.

'That's Enough For Me' is a frenzied rocker with country roots and blues changes.

Lindsey Buckingham: 'Rockabilly on acid. An attempt to do something quite surreal, grounded in something recognizable. I was tapping into a general set of reference points on this album. But I never thought of it in terms of nostalgia. It was anti-nostalgia if you will'.

Likewise, 'Walk A Thin Line' (or 'Song #3') was started in October 1978 but not finished until April 1979.

Two of Buckingham's home-recorded versions of 'Save Me A Place' – dated 10 October and 18 October 1978 – can be heard on the reissue of *Tusk*. This would be recorded by the full band the following March.

'Sara'
Stevie Nicks' 'Sara' is either named after her best friend Sara Recor – who later married Mick Fleetwood – or it was the name she gave to her and

Don Henley's unborn child before she had an abortion in 1977.

Or both.

In a 1991 interview with *GQ*, Henley stated: 'I believe, to the best of my knowledge, she became pregnant by me. And she named the kid Sara, and she had an abortion and then wrote the song of the same name to the spirit of the aborted baby. I was building my house at the time, and there's a line in the song that says, 'And when you build your house, call me''.

Nicks, who was furious that Henley made this public, confirmed the story in 2014, speaking to *Billboard* magazine. 'Had I married Don and had that baby, and had she been a girl, I would have named her Sara.'

The hit version started as a sixteen-minute demo recorded at Studio D in the second week of December 1978: this is the famous 'I don't want to be a cleaning lady!' version, recorded by Stevie with bassist/guitarist Tom Moncrieff, from the Buckingham Nicks band, and vocalist Annie McLoone, who had worked on Walter Egan's *Not Shy* album with Nicks earlier in the year. Nicks played piano, and percussion was provided by a Roland TR-77 drum machine.

For now, 'Sara' was left in its embryonic state. Nicks took the opportunity to record some other new songs, including 'How Still My Love?', 'Outside The Rain' and 'Blue Water'. She would return to all of these in her solo career.

A few days later, Mick Fleetwood added live drums to 'Sara'. The master tape was edited to thirteen minutes for the addition of John McVie's bass. A nine-minute version of the song at this stage of evolution can be heard on the 2004 and 2015 expanded editions of *Tusk*. Neither Tom Moncrieff nor Annie McLoone are credited.

'It was our version that Fleetwood Mac used by overdubbing on top of what we had done', Moncrieff says. 'What appeared on *Tusk* had my acoustic guitars. When they put out the expanded edition, they included a mix of the original demo that included my bass and Annie's vocals. I have no idea why we were never given any credit.'

The song was edited further for Christine McVie's overdubbed piano (in the final version, Nicks' piano is in the left stereo channel, McVie's on the right). Lindsey Buckingham provided layers of acoustic and electric guitar, including an unhinged solo. Lush backing vocals were also added. Ultimately the album version was 6:22. The single version was cut to 4:41 by leaving out the middle verse and instrumental bridge.

1979

'Not That Funny' and 'I Know I'm Not Wrong'

Lindsay Buckingham had continued working on his home recordings during the previous few months. Now, six months into sessions for *Tusk*, and with Stevie Nicks and Christine McVie taking a break, it was time to focus on embellishing and polishing his contributions.

'Not That Funny' is a three-chord thrash with an aggressive, raw attitude quite at odds with, say, 'Over And Over' or 'Sisters Of The Moon'. Featuring de-tuned guitars, an uninhabited vocal and a very compressed 'lo-fi' sound, 'Not That Funny' was quite unlike any other song released under the Fleetwood Mac name.

'I Know I'm Not Wrong' would be developed from one of many home recordings.

"I Know I'm Not Wrong' is a song that featured Lindsey playing most of the instruments, including that raucous harmonica', says assistant engineer, Hernan Rojas. 'Some of the drum parts were doubled and tripled, sort of a 'wall of sound treatment', Phil Spector type. The idea was to get a raw and straightforward sound and performance.'

Co-producer, Ken Caillat, said:

The songs on *Tusk*, Lindsey's songs, I didn't really like any of them because they were filled with such distortion. At one point, I thought we're going to have to put all the speaker-breaking stuff on side four. In contrast, the girls' stuff was so amazing, and I noticed all of his guitar work on the girls' stuff was beautiful. It was some of the best you ever heard. He's so good stuffing frosting into these little cracks in the song, making it sweeter. So we'd always have him part of it. He didn't want any of that in his other songs, 'Not That Funny', and other stuff. I think he did it just to annoy me.

Buckingham said in 1980:

You have to allow yourself to get totally drawn into the music. Once you're there, the hardest thing to do is let yourself do anything outside that. I'd come out of my basement studio after about six hours, and Carol, my girlfriend, would be sitting in the living room watching TV or something, and I just wouldn't have much to say. My mind would be racing. I love it.

'Tusk'

'When Fleetwood Mac was on tour, the band didn't always get a soundcheck before the show', writes Ken Caillat. 'When this happened (they) would always perform a cool warm-up piece that began with Mick playing a low, contagious jungle beat (to which) Lindsey added a funky guitar riff and which John McVie straddled by accenting the riff and locking into the drums for a propulsive groove.'

Thus was born 'Tusk': Fleetwood Mac's first song to reach the top ten in both the UK and US. Initially, this piece of music was known simply as the 'Stage Riff'.

'We transferred Lindsey's sixteen-track home recordings to a clean piece of 24-track tape on the Studer', Ken Caillat recalled. 'The demo we first heard had a drum loop in place and Lindsey's highly reverbed acoustic guitar playing the riff. He sang nonsense syllables with only 'Why don't you ask him if he's going to stay' as the only discernible lyric, with no mention of the word 'tusk'.'

This demo can be heard on the 2015 extended reissue of *Tusk*, dated 15 January 1979. The value that Fleetwood Mac's peerless rhythm section added to songs like 'Tusk', can be appreciated by comparing this demo with an outtake version from a week later: 23 January 1979. Not only do Mick Fleetwood's drums propel the song (helped by some studio trickery of looping an eleven-second, four-bar section), but John McVie's bass line wraps itself around the beat.

'Tusk', at this stage, was weird and fun in equal measures. More – very important – overdubs would be added in June.

'Never Make Me Cry' and 'Think About Me'

Christine McVie's striking 'Never Make Me Cry' is a love letter to Dennis Wilson. It was initially recorded on grand piano and acoustic guitar – just like 'Songbird'. An early take from 8 February is on the 2015 reissue of *Tusk*. Over the next few weeks, Lindsey Buckingham overhauled the song, replacing the grand piano with multiple airy guitar overdubs to build a lush, relaxed sound. An early mix from the 17 April version retains some of the original piano track.

'Think About Me' was started – like 'Never Make Me Cry' – in mid-February. It was recorded in just four takes as an in-your-face band performance with a real live, spontaneous feel: a close cousin to 'Say You Love Me'. This basic take is included on the 2015 reissue of *Tusk*. The final version adds some *Rumours*-era backing vocals and a short 'Go Your Own Way' guitar solo.

Rolling Stone in 2019:

> The millions of people who bought *Tusk* hoping for a follow-up to
> *Rumours* that sounded like its predecessor could breathe a sigh of relief
> when they got to its third song, 'Think About Me', Christine's bright
> pop-rock ode to a no-pressure relationship. '(Stevie and I) didn't really
> like (*Tusk*),' McVie admitted in a recent interview. 'We just kind of went,
> 'O-kaaay.' Because it was so different from *Rumours*. Deliberately so. In
> hindsight, I do like that record, but at the time, me and Stevie would be
> like, 'What the hell is he doing in the toilet playing an empty Kleenex box
> for a drum?'.

'What Makes You Think You're The One?'

The furious 'What Makes You Think You're The One?' (aka 'Lindsey's Song
#6') was recorded as a trio: bass, drums and piano, the latter played by
the song's writer, Lindsey Buckingham. It seems to be a message to Stevie
Nicks – Buckingham's bleating vocal and rudimentary piano-playing must
surely be a dig at his ex-girlfriend. An early mix, dated 24 February 1979,
is on the expanded reissue of *Tusk*.

Buckingham recalled to *Uncut*:

> We were really looking to get some kind of crazy drum sound. That was
> back in the day when everybody had boom boxes, and we had an old
> cassette player with these really crappy mics. But you could record on it,
> and the system had built-in compressors, and we took the output. We put
> that right in front of the drums, and I think we put another one overhead,
> too, as opposed to mic'ing the whole thing as you usually do. And we ran
> that cassette player into the console and it just made this really explosive,
> trashy sound. That's one of the great drum tracks that I've ever heard.
> That's up there with 'Instant Karma.' That was a great moment. There
> was a 'fuck you' thing about it on some level. Not directed at anybody in
> particular but at the business, the need to conform to some vague set of
> commercial standards. That was Mick and myself late at night in the studio,
> me at the piano. Mick turned into an animal. There (wasn't) anybody
> putting any constraints on what could or couldn't be done. That has to rate
> as one of my top-five moments in the band.

'It is the sound of the barbarians at the gates', suggests Ken Caillat. 'With
a martial drum beat built around the snare and kick, and straight-ahead

ham-fisted piano chords that just pounded the song's vindictive lyrics forward like a battering ram.'

Night Eyes

Caillat had produced an album for L.A. band, The Big Wha-Koo, in 1978. Singer and guitarist Danny Douma recorded a solo album, *Night Eyes*, the following year, but it was not a hit, despite the presence of most of Fleetwood Mac and Eric Clapton on lead guitar on one track. Douma toured with Fleetwood Mac as a support act on the *Tusk* tour.

'Save Me A Place' and 'The Dealer'

Work recommenced on 'Save Me A Place': an acoustic song reminiscent of the best work of Neil Young. Buckingham sings all the vocal parts himself. This Studio D version is intimate and forlorn. It's a highlight of *Tusk*. A version of Stevie Nicks' song, 'The Dealer', was recorded at around this time, although it was never completed to the band's satisfaction. This recording has never been released. Ken Caillat:

> When we start an album, we have every intention of using every song. However, you never know how well they will turn out. I think Stevie decided she would like to use that song on her own album.

'The Farmer's Daughter'

A studio version of The Beach Boys', 'The Farmer's Daughter', dates from this period.

Jon Stebbins discussed it in *The Real Beach Boy – Dennis Wilson:*

> One night, while Lindsay Buckingham and Stevie Nicks were working at Village Recorders, Dennis, Christine, and Ed Roach stopped by. 'We all started talking about Brian,' remembers Roach. 'Stevie and Lindsey were saying what big Beach Boys fans they were when they were teenagers.' Then, in a casual a cappella style, Buckingham and Nicks started singing Brian's old song 'The Farmer's Daughter' from *Surfin´ USA*. Dennis teased Christine, saying, 'See, I told you we were good.' At that point, Dennis and Ed left the studio to paint the town. In the early morning hours, they returned, worn out, to pick up Christine. 'We knocked on the studio door and Christine unlocked it to let us in,' recalls Roach. 'She had tears running down her face and said, 'My God, I was hoping it was you guys!'. When Dennis asked, 'What's the matter? Are we late?' Christine just led them

quietly back into the studio. She wanted them to hear what had made her so emotional. Lindsey, Stevie and Christine, all fighting tears, played back the arrangement of 'The Farmer's Daughter' they had been working on all night. 'Dennis freaked out when he heard it, and he started crying too,' says Roach. A short time later, their beautiful rendition of Brian's classic song would reach a whole new audience as a cut on a Fleetwood Mac live album.

This was released on *Fleetwood Mac Live* in 1980, where it is listed as 'recorded at Santa Monica Civic Auditorium (for crew and friends)'. This is a white lie. The recording sessions for 'Farmer's Daughter' are described in some detail in the book, *Get Tusked*, published in 2019. Comparison of this studio version – included on the 2004 version of *Tusk* – with the 1980 'live' release prove that they are the exact same recording. The 2004 release simply fades about 10 seconds earlier.

'The Beach Boys showed the way, and not just to California', Buckingham wrote in a piece for *Rolling Stone*. 'They may have sold the California dream to a lot of people, but for me, it was Brian Wilson showing how far you might have to go in order to make your own musical dream come true.'

Buckingham said in 1981:

I've always been a Brian Wilson fan. And so much of what he's done has either gone over people's heads or been ignored for one reason or another. A lot of people stopped buying Beach Boys records when Brian stopped writing about surfing, and that's a shame. There are a lot of great Brian songs that were never hits. 'Farmer's Daughter' probably could've been a successful single for them if they'd released it. I think 'Surfin' USA' was the only real hit from that album. But I've loved 'Farmer's Daughter'. It's obscure enough that I thought it would be good for us to cover. I think it would be a great single.

Fleetwood Mac's cover of 'Farmer's Daughter' would indeed be released as a single in spring 1981.

'Angel'
The last new song started for *Tusk* was Nicks' 'Angel'. 'Angel' takes its rhythm and tempo directly from Warren Zevon's 'Werewolves Of London'.

'I wanted to record a rock and roll song', Nicks said. 'And so it started out being much sillier than it came out. It didn't end up being silly at all, actually. But when I started it, I thought, for me, because I write so many intense, serious, dark songs, that I wanted to write something that was 'up'. But there's a definite eeriness that goes through that song too.'

'Angel' was recorded in six takes by the full band.

At around the same time: April 1979, Lindsey Buckingham returned to 'Walk A Thin Line' – which had been started the previous October – adding grand piano (recorded at half-speed), Ovation acoustic guitars, sustained electric guitar chords, multiple drum tracks and an out-of-phase rock choir. If 'That's Enough For Me is 'rockabilly on acid', then 'Walk A Thin Line' is doo-wop on Klonopin. Listen to the song now, out of context from the rest of the album – it's utterly fabulous.

Mick Fleetwood recorded a version of 'Walk A Thin Line' on his 1981 debut solo album, *The Visitor*. A certain G. Harrison of Arnold Grove, Liverpool, plays slide guitar and twelve-string guitar.

Towards the end of the sessions, Lindsey Buckingham took delivery of a handsome, new, hand-built guitar: the Rick Turner Model One. Buckingham used this on the *Tusk* tour, *The Dance*, and many of his solo albums.

'I got to know Lindsey Buckingham and the band when they were recording *Rumours* in Sausalito', Turner says. 'John McVie was using, and buying, Alembic basses, and I was working on Lindsey's guitars. Lindsey and I have similar musical roots. He plays with his fingers, not a flat pick; he's basically an acoustic player gone electric. Me too. So the idea of designing a guitar that would feel right to an acoustic player would deliver the kind of detailed tone that you get from a fine acoustic, but then be able to go toe-to-toe with any Les Paul, but maintain more of the clarity of a Strat: that was the goal.'

May 1979

May was spent taking stock, mixing and overdubbing.

The album was given its title at around this time. Stevie Nicks recalled to *Mojo* in 2015: 'I didn't understand the title, there was nothing beautiful or elegant about the word 'tusk'. It really brought to mind those people stealing ivory. Even then, in 1979, you just thought the rhinos are being poached and that tusks are being stolen and the elephants are being slaughtered and ivory is being sold on the black market. I don't recall it being (Mick's slang term for the male member); that went right over my prudish little head. I wasn't told that until quite a while after the record was done, and when I did find out, I liked the title even less!'.

The artwork and packaging was in development. The cover image shows Ken Caillat's dog, Scooter. 'My dog is biting my leg', he said. 'I think they only liked it because they could see his canine.'

There was also some extracurricular activity. After producing big hits for Bob Welch and Walter Egan in 1977 and 1978, Lindsey Buckingham helped produce three top 40 singles for John Stewart in 1979, on the recommendation of Walter Egan. Stewart had been a member of The Kingston Trio, wrote 'Daydream Believer' for The Monkees, and was a big influence on Buckingham.

Lindsay Buckingham:

> With John Stewart, it just seemed like the right thing to do at (that) particular time. I'm real good at editing out this section or saying, 'Let's do this in here'. That's the thing I'm probably best at – being able to think abstractly and say, 'This isn't making it here; let's do this; put this part in here, and it'll make all the difference in the world'. But choosing to do that as a whole project is something that I don't do very often. On *Bombs Away Dream Babies*, I wasn't in the studio with John as much as I would have liked to have been because we were working on *Tusk* at the time. It kind of blew John's mind when I first met him, because I knew all his songs.

Stevie Nicks sang on the album, including its biggest hit, 'Gold', which sounds a lot like a pumped up 'Sisters Of The Moon' with the guitar solo from 'The Chain'. We should also note here the rough-and-ready version of Jorge Calderon's 'Kiss and Run' that was recorded at some stage in the *Tusk* sessions and is included in the 2004 reissue.

4 June 1979: The Spirit of Troy

Mick Fleetwood: 'I came up with the idea of using the brass band on 'Tusk', and using about 100 drummers on it. (The rest of Fleetwood Mac) thought for sure I'm 'round the twist, and I said, 'Well, I'm going to pay for it. And we're going to film it'. They thought, 'He's blown it. He's way off the deep end''.

For this vital, inventive and unique element to the album's title track, Fleetwood employed the marching band of the University of Southern California, the Spirit of Troy. They were recorded outdoors and marching on the spot at Dodger Stadium on 4 June 1979. The Los Angeles Dodgers baseball team were on a road trip.

It was 'the largest one and a half minutes overdub in pop music history' suggests co-producer, Ken Caillat. The score was written and conducted by the band's director, Dr Arthur C Bartner: a position he held for fifty years, from 1970 until the end of 2020.

The sessions were also filmed, but John McVie was absent, replaced by a life-size cardboard cutout. 'I'd just sailed from L.A. to Tahiti', he said many years later, 'and was hanging out down there. The cardboard cutout seemed like a good idea to me. Wish I could have done that in all of the videos'.

Gretchen Heffler of the Spirit of Troy recalls, 'We had a rehearsal on campus beforehand. Mick Fleetwood came in, worked with the percussion, worked with us. 'This is how it's supposed to go…'. And we were like, 'This really is going to be interesting'. When we got to Dodger Stadium, we pretty much knew what to do'.

Two in-progress mixes of the song at this stage of its development were released on the 2015 expanded reissue of *Tusk*.

Polishing and Mixing

Overdubs and mixing sessions continued through June, July, August and September 1979. The songs mixed, and the dates the basic tracks were recorded are:

> June 1978: 'Can't Walk Out Of Here' (later 'The Ledge'), 'Come On, Baby' (later 'Never Forget')
> September-October 1978: 'Sisters Of The Moon', 'Brown Eyes', 'That's All For Everyone', 'Storms', 'Beautiful Child', 'Over And Over', 'Honey Hi', 'That's Enough For Me', 'Walk A Thin Line'
> December 1978: 'Sara'
> January 1979: 'Not That Funny', 'I Know I'm Not Wrong', 'Tusk'
> February 1979: 'Never Make Me Cry', 'Think About Me', 'What Makes You Think You're The One?'
> March 1979: 'Save Me A Place', 'Farmer's Daughter'
> April 1979: 'Angel'

The completed album included six songs by Christine McVie, nine by Lindsey Buckingham and five by Stevie Nicks.

McVie's 'Over And Over' is immaculately produced, dreamy, and sounds amazing on headphones – especially Buckingham's gorgeous slide guitar. It's perhaps too slow as an opening track, but one cannot fault its craft. 'Think About Me' is pure *Rumours* and is the welcome sound of all five members playing together, as is 'Honey Hi', although the latter feels curiously incomplete. The backing vocals are lovely, however – this might have made a relaxed ending to side four of the original album. 'Brown

Eyes' is blissfully relaxed and reserved, with a quirky drum track and backing vocals worthy of 'I'm Not In Love'. The alternative mix on the expanded reissue of *Tusk* has much more of Peter Green's lead guitar, which can only be heard clearly in the closing seconds of the original version. 'Never Forget' is a mid-tempo rocker, perhaps too polite for its own good. The short but perfect 'Never Make Me Cry' is a masterpiece that owes as much to Lindsey Buckingham's production work as to Chris McVie's singing and songwriting. The early mix on the expanded *Tusk* clearly shows how much Buckingham worked to improve this song in moving from a keeper to a classic.

Buckingham's contributions range from simply utterly uncompromising to quite brilliant: sometimes in the same song. 'The Ledge' sets out his stall for *Tusk*. Harsh, loud and quirky but definitely out of place. Which was the point, after all. 'What Makes You Think You're The One' has a first-take feel and has the fewest overdubs of any of the songs on the album: scintillating guitar slashes. It does become tiresome, though, as does 'Not That Funny', which *is* funny, if overlong and harsh: it's not softened by backing vocals or keyboards. The brilliant 'Save Me A Place' is simple, raw and full of melancholic self-pity: it's a first-rate song. Equally good is 'That's All For Everyone', which washes past in a glory of sound – like Genesis produced by Brian Wilson. 'Walk A Thin Line' comes close to emulating 'That's All For Everyone' but suffers from a lethargic pace. 'That's Enough For Me' is a lot of fun, and at 1:50, is long enough. 'I Know I'm Not Wrong' follows the same path as 'The Ledge' and 'That's Enough for Me': a good song in isolation, with some sprightly guitars, but unfulfilling. 'Tusk' is perhaps the most unorthodox track by a major artist to make the top ten in both the US and the UK. It is – whisper it – a novelty song.

Nicks' striking 'Sara' re-works 'Dreams'. It was a crucial second hit single from the album. Fleetwood's ambitious and masterful drums, snap and rumble as Nicks chants the ambiguously atmospheric and sexy lyrics ('He was just like a great dark wing/Within the wings of a storm/I think I had met my match'). The production is astounding – listen on headphones, the backing harmonies are as lush as you like. Nicks' solo career was just around the corner. 'Storms' is a slow, delicate ballad that was harshly programmed immediately after 'What Makes You Think You're The One' at the end of side one. Listen to this one out of sequence for the depth of production and for Nicks' voice audibly breaking on, 'So I try to say goodbye my friend/I'd like to leave you with something warm/But never have I been a blue calm sea /I have always been a storm'. 'Sisters Of The Moon' is another of Nicks' moody, mystical hymns, with wonderful dynamics and a truly outstanding performance from Lindsey Buckingham. 'Beautiful Child' is very slow, almost pedestrian, but utilises Nicks' simple chord sequence and rising dynamics to brilliant effect. Buckingham and McVie's backing vocals increase in fulfilling complexity. 'Angel' is Nicks' weakest on the album, despite the welcome harmonies in the chorus.

In 1979, a double studio album was a statement. Since Johnny's Cash's *Sings the Ballads of the True West* (1965), Bob Dylan's *Blonde on Blonde* and The Mothers of Invention's *Freak Out!* (both 1966), major artists with either 'something to say' or simply a glut of new material, released such diverse and/or successful albums as *Electric Ladyland* (1968), *The Beatles* (aka the *'White Album'*) (1968), *Tommy* (1969), *Trout Mask Replica* (1969), *Bitches Brew* (1970), *Third* (1970), *All Things Must Pass* (1970, a triple), *Layla and Other Assorted Love Songs* (1970), *Something/Anything* (1972), *Exile on Main Street* (1972), *Living in the Past* (1972), *Manassas* (1972), *Quadrophenia* (1973), *Tales from Topographic Oceans* (1973), *Goodbye Yellow Brick Road* (1973), *The Lamb Lies Down on Broadway* (1974), *Metal Machine Music* (1975), *Physical Graffiti* (1975), *Songs in the Key of Life* (1976), *Don Juan's Reckless Daughter* (1977), *Out of the Blue* (1977) and *Here My Dear* (1978).

It's possible that all of these albums could be tightened up by removing two or three songs, but none can be successfully trimmed to a 40-minute single album without losing the heart of the artists' visions. As for *Tusk*, even if we snip, say, 'Never Forget', 'The Ledge', 'What Makes You Think You're The One', 'Walk A Thin Line', 'I Know I'm Not Wrong' and 'Angel', we still have fourteen songs and 53 minutes of music.

The issue is perhaps not so much too many songs but jarring sequencing. This was, of course, a deliberate decision by the producers: Dashut, Caillat and Buckingham.

'We had to imagine a running order that would cohere and sound good', Caillat wrote later, 'taking into consideration tempo, genre, vibe, tone, singer, and potential intertextual dialogues, such as the segue from 'Sara' to 'What Makes You Think You're The One' to 'Storms''.

But the gentle 'Storms' suffers, coming immediately after the raucous 'What Makes You Think You're The One'; 'I Know I'm Not Wrong' devilishly punctures the mood after 'Never Make Me Cry', and overpowers the song that follows, 'Honey Hi'.

Lindsey Buckingham called it a 'study in contrasts'. Here's an alternative playing sequence.

Side one: 'Tusk', 'Over And Over', 'Save Me A Place', 'Sara', 'That's All For Everyone'
Side two: 'Think About Me', 'Storms', 'Sisters Of The Moon', 'The Ledge', 'What Makes You Think You're The One'
Side three: 'Never Make Me Cry', 'That's Enough For Me', 'I Know I'm Not Wrong', 'Not That Funny', 'Walk A Thin Line'
Side four: 'Angel', 'Brown Eyes', 'Beautiful Child', 'Never Forget', 'Honey Hi'

Either way, *Tusk* shows a depth and maturity of both production and performance that listeners today will appreciate. Most of the songs on *Rumours* have been played to death on the radio for the last forty years. The songs on *Tusk* are less familiar and sound much fresher. Listen again to this album: there's lots to enjoy.

Tusk Lands

'Tusk', the single, was released in September 1979. It surprised many people by reaching the top ten in both the UK and the US: the first of only three Fleetwood Mac singles to achieve that momentous feat (the others were Buckingham's 'Big Love' and Christine McVie's 'Little Lies').

Rolling Stone had this to say in 2019:

A landmark of badass rock and roll bravado: The world's most popular group, after perfecting an L.A. rock formula that went mega-platinum around the world, decided to rip it up and start again. 'Tusk' sounded like commercial suicide – yet it turned into one of the weirdest Top Ten hits any megastars ever dropped. Buckingham and co-producer Richard Dashut took a drum riff that Fleetwood devised to warm up before shows and looped it into an evil-sounding sex-and-drugs chant, with the singers practically whispering, 'Why won't you tell me who's on the phone?' Halfway through, it explodes into a free-for-all rock jam. Not weird enough? They added the USC Marching Band, inspired by a brass band Fleetwood saw at a village festival in France. It was excess in every sense of the word.

The album followed a couple of weeks later. Robert Christgau – who'd given *Rumours* an A grade in his *Village Voice Consumer Guide* – lowered his rating to B+ for *Tusk*.

Not only don't Lindsey Buckingham's swelling edges and dynamic separations get in the way of the music, they're inextricable from the music, or maybe they are the music. The passionate dissociation of the mix is entirely appropriate to an ensemble in which the three principals have all but disappeared (vocally) from each other's work. But only Buckingham is attuned enough to get exciting music out of a sound so spare and subtle, it reveals the limits of Christine McVie's simplicity and shows Stevie Nicks up for the mooncalf she's always been.

Stephen Holden said this in *Rolling Stone* on 13 December 1979:

At a cost of two years and well over a million dollars, Fleetwood Mac's *Tusk* represents both the last word in lavish California studio pop and a brave but tentative lurch forward by the one Seventies group that can claim a musical chemistry as mysteriously right – though not as potent – as the Beatles'. In its fits and starts and restless changes of pace, *Tusk* inevitably recalls the Beatles' *White Album* (1968): the quirky rock jigsaw puzzle that showed the Fab Four at their artiest and most indecisive.

Like the *White Album*, *Tusk* is less a collection of finished songs than a mosaic of pop-rock fragments by individual performers. Tusk's twenty tunes constitute a two-record 'trip' that covers a lot of ground, from rock and roll basics to a shivery psychedelia reminiscent of the band's earlier *Bare Trees* and *Future Games* to the opulent extremes of folk-rock arcana given the full Hollywood treatment. The *White Album* was also a trip, but one that reflected the furious social banging around at the end of the Sixties. Tusk is much vaguer. Semi-programmatic and non-literary, it ushers out the Seventies with a long, melancholy sigh.

Tusk finds Fleetwood Mac slightly tipsy from jet lag and fine wine, teetering about in the late-afternoon sun and making exquisite small talk. Surely, they must all be aware of the evanescence of the golden moment that this album has captured so majestically.

Tusk would spend nine months in the US charts, peaking at number four. Mick Fleetwood maintains that sales were knocked significantly by Westwood One's broadcast of the entire album on the day of release.

That might be true; the high price tag of over $15 won't have helped. Nevertheless, two million copies of a double album are nothing to sneeze at. In the UK, *Tusk* would hit number one in November 1979, three weeks into a 21-week run.

'The rest of the band had a cynical view towards the way *Tusk* was made and the reasons why I thought it was important to move into new territory', Lindsey Buckingham recalls. 'It wasn't just negativity. There was open hostility. Then I got a certain amount of flak because it didn't sell as many as *Rumours*. Mick would say to me, 'Well, you went too far, you blew it'. That hurt. And so it's gratifying now to hear Mick tell anyone who asks, that it's his favourite Fleetwood Mac album.'

'*Tusk* is probably my favourite and most important Fleetwood Mac album', Mick Fleetwood said. '*Tusk* meant this band's survival – if we hadn't made that album, we might have broken up.'

'How am I supposed to interpret *Tusk* selling so many fewer copies (than *Rumours)?*', Lindsey Buckingham later asked himself. 'I just can't take it too seriously. Sales are not necessarily indicative of quality.'

In 2003, American band, Camper Van Beethoven, recorded a song-by-song remake of *Tusk*. In an interview with the *Chicago Tribune*, bass player Victor Krummenacher said that the album was 'like the *Magnificent Ambersons* of rock, a work that's supposed to be good, but is really just a cocaine-damaged horror of excess. Which is why we took it on, I suppose, and I think we improved upon it'.

Two expanded reissues add many alternative mixes, unused songs and incomplete demos. An alternative version of 'Brown Eyes' and alternative mixes of 'Beautiful Child' and 'Tusk', are available on *25 Years – The Chain*.

Tusk Tour

Fleetwood Mac booked SIR Studio for six weeks of rehearsals, ahead of another huge tour.

Mick Fleetwood: 'We set out on a year-long tour of North America, the Pacific and Europe, in support of *Tusk*'.

That tour began on 26 October 1979 and comprised 112 dates through to September 1980. Their setlist was 'Say You Love Me', 'The Chain', 'Dreams', 'Not That Funny', 'Rhiannon', 'Over And Over' (or 'Don't Stop'), 'Oh Well', 'Sara', 'What Makes You Think You're The One', 'Oh Daddy' (or 'Sara'), 'Save Me A Place', 'Landslide', 'Tusk', 'Angel', 'You Make Loving Fun', 'I'm So Afraid', 'World Turning', 'Go Your Own Way',

'Sisters Of The Moon', 'Blue Letter' and 'Songbird'. Live performances of 'The Ledge' and 'Save Me A Place' would feature Christine McVie on acoustic guitar.

Mick Fleetwood says:

In my opinion, this was the very height of our touring at the top of excess. We had a team of karate experts as our security guards, a full-time Japanese masseuse, our catering was supplied by top-notch California chefs, and it usually went uneaten. We had our own airliner and we booked the best hotel suites in the world. We had rooms in those hotels repainted in advance of our arrival. We had a huge cocaine budget.

Many of the dates were recorded. 'Oh Well' and 'Sara' – recorded 5 November 1979 at the Checkerdome in St. Louis – are on *Fleetwood Mac Live*, released December 1980. Live versions of 'Over And Over', 'Not That Funny', 'Save Me A Place', 'Tusk', 'What Makes You Think You're The One' and 'Angel' from this concert are available on the five-disc reissue of *Tusk*. The entire show from 6 November at the same venue is available in pristine sound quality on bootleg.

The Spirit of Troy performed 'Tusk' with the band on five dates at the Forum in Inglewood, CA.

14-16 December 1979, Cow Palace, San Francisco

Dressed in a black shirt and a plain gray suit, his hair cropped short, Lindsey Buckingham is pacing the stage of San Francisco's Cow Palace. The guitarist clearly stands out from the rest of the band, both musically and visually. Whether he is singing one of his own songs from the new Tusk album or backing Nicks or McVie on one of their tunes, Buckingham plays and looks like a man possessed – his fixed stare never leaving the audience, a sinister grin never leaving his face. With three rim shots from Fleetwood's snare drum and a piano glissando from Christine McVie, Buckingham shouts, 'What makes you think you're the one', pointing at his ex-girlfriend Stevie Nicks. As has come to be expected, the set's highpoint is 'I'm So Afraid', a tour de force study in dynamics with Lindsey Buckingham's echoing guitar building in speed, volume and intensity.
(*Musician Magazine* No.33, June 1981)

Postscript: 1980 And Beyond

The *Tusk* tour ended on 1 September 1980. Fleetwood Mac were physically and mentally drained and barely able to stand the sight of each other.

'I used to go onstage and drink a bottle of Dom Perignon, and drink one offstage afterwards', Christine McVie later recalled. 'It's not the kind of party I'd like to go to now. There was a lot of booze being drunk and there was blood floating around in the alcohol, which doesn't make for a stable environment.'

'Not That Funny' – an unlikely single in the UK, Germany and the Netherlands in March 1980 – did not chart. In the US, 'Think About Me' crept into the top 20. 'Sisters Of The Moon' was a single in June 1980, as was 'Farmer's Daughter' from the *Tusk* sessions, the following year.

Once the tour was over, the band was put on hold. Stevie Nicks went straight into the studio to record her hugely successful *Bella Donna* album between Autumn 1980 and Spring 1981. Buckingham started on his first solo album, *Law and Order*, recorded over several months from late 1980. Fleetwood's *The Visitor* was laid down in January and February 1981.

The classic line-up of Fleetwood Mac recorded two more albums. *Mirage* (1982) was lacklustre but contained the big hits 'Oh Diane', 'Hold Me' and 'Gypsy'. 1987's *Tango in the Night* provided another three huge hit singles. But Lindsey Buckingham did not want to go on tour, as he told *Uncut* in 2003:

> When I was done with the record, I said, 'Oh my God. That was the worst recording experience of my life'. And compared to making an album, in my experience, going on the road will multiply the craziness by times five. I just wasn't up for that. I needed to pull out of the machine and try to maintain a level of integrity for the work that wasn't about the scale or the sales.

Undeterred, two new guitar players replaced him for the Shake the Cage tour: 69 shows from September 1987 to June 1988. This line-up recorded *Behind the Mask* in 1989-1990 (a number 1 in the UK) and toured the world once more from March to December 1990.

The Buckingham/Nicks/McVie/McVie/Fleetwood line-up reunited in 1993 at the request of Bill Clinton for his first inaugural ball.

And then… if Fleetwood Mac without Lindsey Buckingham was hard to imagine, try Fleetwood Mac without Stevie Nicks or Christine McVie. The *Time* line-up and tour (1994-1995) is best forgotten. Stevie Nicks, meanwhile, spent 47 days in the Daniel Freeman hospital in Marina del Rey, kicking a debilitating prescription tranquilliser habit.

The classic five-piece reunited on a sound stage at Burbank Studios on 22 May 1997. The live album, *The Dance*, took Fleetwood Mac back to the top of the US album charts for the first time in 10 years. The album sold five million copies and kept Fleetwood Mac on the road throughout much of 1997. Christine McVie retired following the tour and live performances at the Rock and Roll Hall of Fame induction and the 1998 Grammy Awards. The band's seventeenth and to date last album, *Say You Will*, was released in 2003. They toured extensively in 2003-2004 and again in 2009 and 2013, the latter accompanied by a four-song EP.

Much to the surprise of many, Christine McVie returned to Fleetwood Mac in 2014, performing shows with the 1975-1987 line-up across the world in 2014 and 2015. Studio sessions followed. These were released – after Stevie Nicks chose not to contribute – as *Lindsey Buckingham/ Christine McVie* in 2017.

And then Lindsey Buckingham was summarily fired from Fleetwood Mac. A lawsuit followed. Former Tom Petty and the Heartbreakers guitarist Mike Campbell and Neil Finn of Crowded House replaced him, and this nineteenth official line-up of Fleetwood Mac performed 88 shows between October 2018 and November 2019.

As 2021 ends, Mick Fleetwood is 74; John McVie, 75; Christine McVie, 78; Lindsey Buckingham, 72; and Stevie Nicks, 73.

Peter Green, Bob Brunning, Bob Welch, Danny Kirwan and Bob Weston are dead.

What the future holds is anyone's guess.

Bibliography

Brackett, D., *Fleetwood Mac: 40 Years of Creative Chaos* (Praeger, Westport, 2007)

Brunning, B., *The Fleetwood Mac Story: Rumours and Lies* (Omnibus Press, London, 1990/1998/2004)

Caillat, K. and Stiefel, S., *Making Rumours: The Inside Story of the Classic Fleetwood Mac Album* (John Wiley and Sons, Hoboken, 2013)

Caillat, K. and Rojas, H., *Get Tusked: The Inside Story of Fleetwood Mac's Most Anticipated Album* (Backbeat Books, Lanham, 2019)

Cresswell, T. and Mathieson, C., *The 100 Best Albums of All Time* (Hardie Grant, London, 2013)

Davis, S., *Gold Dust Woman: The Biography of Stevie Nicks* (St. Martin's Press, London, 2017)

Fleetwood, M. and Bozza, A., *Play On: Now, Then, and Fleetwood Mac* (Little Brown, London, 2014)

Frame, P., *Even More Rock Family Trees* (Omnibus Press, London, 2011)

Graham, S., *Fleetwood Mac, The Authorised History* (Warner Bros Publications, Los Angeles, 1978)

Harris, C. A., *Storms: My Life with Lindsey Buckingham and Fleetwood Mac* (Chicago Review Press, Chicago, 2007)

Lewry, P., *Fleetwood Mac: The Complete Recording Sessions 1967-1997* (Blandford, London, 1998)

Price, B., *Making the Turner Guitar* (The Association of Stringed Instruments Artisans, New York, 1994)

Rooksby, R., *The Complete Guide to the Music of Fleetwood Mac* (Omnibus Books, London, 1998)

Trucks, R., *Fleetwood Mac's Tusk* (Continuum, New York, 2011)

Unterberger, R., *Fleetwood Mac: The Complete Illustrated History* (Voyageur Press, Beverley, 2016)